Upon the shores your whispers roll

Amongst the wind your courage strolls

The weight you carry through loveless seas

Released by wings of angels freed.

-My dearest grandma Iris, aka Mother Sam, I heard your prayers then and I feel them stronger than ever now.

Thank you for believing.

GREETINGS ...

When I was directed to this assignment I had no idea that it would be such a task. I am what most would call an expert in my field, but this particular job did not require my expertise. Instead, it required uncommon faith. Faith and faith alone was the only way out of the storm that brewed viciously ahead. My name is Cor, Angel of Love, and I specialize in broken hearts. I do not have the power to mend them, but I have been given the authority to prevent them as I thought I would with this assignment. I am well aware that each assignment is unique, but this one… this one was far different from any other. My assignment had been destined for greatness prior to her birth and it was my job to let her know it. The Destined was a naïve but gentle soul, misguided by life's chaotic misfortunes. Love and life were unreliable to her and she became aware of it at an early age. Her father walked out of her life when she was only seven years old, and that was the day The Destined began to believe that love was an unrealistic fairytale. The absence of her father, whom she loved so deeply, initiated a desperate search for his replacement – someone to love, someone to *love her* unconditionally, and someone to let her know that she was beautiful. Her mother did the best as any single parent could but The Destined thirsted for more. She was thirsty for the love and approval of her father. Unknowingly, all she wanted was to fill the emptiness which once held her father's love. To make her fairytale real, she repeatedly fell for the conniving traps of seduction that apprehended her. I was sent to stop this cycle. It had to end immediately – before it ended her. When The Destined met him, The Charming, a suave, manipulative womanizer, I knew it was time. As an angel, my task is to guide and protect my assignments from the rulers of darkness. But this one, The Destined, she was special. She had something within her, something powerful, and she had to be tested in order for it to shine. For this reason, I could not direct her. While she made her choices, I prepared for war. The battle had begun, and the war was near.

1

THE ROOT

It was common for The Charming to call out of the blue with some crazy spur of the moment idea, so The Destined, Destiny, as he had named her, thought nothing of it. She subconsciously argued with her conscience and convinced herself that it was a good plan.

Destiny was raised in a single parent home. Her mother tried very hard to conceal the stress of being the only provider for four children, but as Destiny grew older she saw right through her mother. Destiny's mother kept her and her siblings well-dressed and introduced them to the finer side of life, but Destiny could remember hearing her mother's sobs from behind her bedroom door some nights. It was then that the struggle became evident. So when The Charming called with the idea, Destiny was convinced. She had her own children now, and she did not want to struggle to take care of them as her mother did. This was an opportunity to support her children financially without always living on a budget. Who wouldn't want that? They needed her to do this for them, they deserved it. This was what she convinced herself of I tried to discourage her thoughts, but she ignored my attempts. Her mind was made up and my mission had begun. There was no way I was leaving her! Not now. Not with him, "The Charming."

I knew he was a bad drift of wind from the day that I met him, with his fancy car and his fancy jewelry. I saw right through him. But not her, absolutely not; she was in love. Hypnotized by an illusion that this carbon copy of a man brought value to her existence, and he knew it.

"Trust me baby girl," he said in a smooth monotone voice as he introduced his proposal. "We need to do this. Once we get past this part, we'll never have to do it again."

Destiny felt her heart beat a little faster as she listened nervously on the other end of the phone.

He continued, "Three months tops, baby girl. That's it. We get there, we get what we need, and we leave. These three months would be like the beginning of the rest of our lives together. Happy and rich!" he laughed.

Destiny smiled. Sometimes, when he spoke, that was all it took. "Well, what would I be doing?" she asked.

"Help me run the business. That's it. I just need you there with me. You know, to help me make decisions and stuff."

Her smile got a little bigger. Her heart was now beating out of her chest, but she ignored it. I screamed as loud as I could, "NO!" but she ignored me too.

"Sure babe," she agreed, "I wouldn't let you do this alone."

Destiny spent the rest of that night trying to soothe her conscience and convince herself that she had made the right decision. With her children huddled in her arms, she laid on the old twin bed where all three of them slept. Her daughter, five years old, was fast asleep with her head positioned deep into the armpit of her mother. Destiny moved a little bit to gain some comfort, but the little girl's head just followed right along. Destiny smiled, and turned to look at her son, who was in her other arm, studying every part of his mother's face with his big brown eyes. His eyelashes were so long that they appeared to get stuck together every time he blinked. "Why are you still awake?" Destiny whispered, stroking the feeding tube that was protruding from his nostrils. He had just turned a year old, but his body was as tiny as a six month old. Destiny had a healthy pregnancy, and there were no complications during his birth, but many health problems began to manifest *after* he was born. He had to be fed through a feeding tube, and was unable to walk, or even crawl. He had to wear a heart monitor around the clock and was unable to respond to noise. He cried, but couldn't make any other sounds that healthy toddlers were able to make. Destiny held her babies a little closer as she thought about all that they had been through, and she blamed herself for every bit of it. They didn't ask to be moved from house to house. They didn't ask for a father that was abusive towards their mother. They didn't ask for any of it!

Her eyes began to fill with tears as she looked back at her daughter and remembered the trauma that even she had endured when Destiny was six months pregnant with her. She remembered the scent of the pillow that smothered her face. She remembered the pillow pressing harder and harder against her face and thinking, 'it's almost over baby', hoping that this thought would somehow be transmitted to her precious child. She remembered the sound of the screeching bed frame and the strong scent of cheap cologne. She remembered hearing guns drawn and her favorite black summer dress being torn as she cradled her stomach, trying to protect her unborn child as she wondered why. She remembered it like it was yesterday.

Destiny was only seventeen when she got pregnant with her first child. She had enlisted into the Air Force and was supposed to join right after graduation in June of 1997. It was the military physical examination that revealed her pregnancy. Destiny was in shock when she found out, and her mother was heartbroken. Her mother had always held Destiny to a high standard, and she endured a very strict upbringing. It seemed as though her father leaving intensified her mother's expectations, so when she found out that Destiny was pregnant, she was devastated. Her mother had warned her about the troubled boyfriend that Destiny was involved with at the time, but Destiny didn't listen. Instead, she continued the relationship and had another child with him, despite the fact that he was a cheating, abusive jailbird. Destiny's mother tried hard to show her love and support for her daughter, but the bitterness of her disappointment was transparent and weakened her relationship with Destiny. Destiny felt like a disappointment, and acted as such. The love was there, but the bond had perished. Destiny's psychological addiction to be mistreated by her so-called *love* ended abruptly when the father of her children was incarcerated for attacking her with a razor blade. Only then did Destiny see the true danger that she was in and snapped into reality. Unfortunately, she was still blinded by the desire to be loved, and carelessly fell once again into the arms of deceit when she fell for, The Charming.

"I have to do this!" she belted out.

Her roommate jumped out her sleep from across the room, "Have to do what?"

"Nothing, I'll tell you tomorrow. Go back to sleep."

The roommate, Destiny's best friend at the time, turned towards the wall and put the baby blue blanket back over her face. This time headphones went under the blanket with her. Destiny went into a trance while staring at the teal painted walls. There were brush marks splashed on the white ceiling where they didn't tape off. Destiny counted every one of them as she calculated her thoughts and slowly drifted to sleep. I tried to reason with her once again, but her thoughts were blocked. Her mind was made up.

2

THE BAIT

"Good morning!" the receptionist at the church daycare said cheerfully, waving at Destiny's little package of two. Her cheeks lit up with joy every time she laid eyes on Destiny and her children. This was indeed a special family. Apparently, I was not the only one that knew it. Destiny had been a member of Faith Tabernacle Church for years now, located on the east end of Houston only ten minutes away from where Destiny was living. Many people noticed the light that she carried within her, but Destiny did not seem to notice it herself. In her mind she was invisible to others, but she was wrong. She was so wrong.

"Good morning Mrs. Debbie!" Destiny responded, flashing her white teeth. Her smile was what she loved the most about herself. Actually, it was the only thing she liked about her physical appearance, in addition to her chocolate brown skin. Destiny was skinny and slender, and in her eyes, as flat as a pancake. Her body was far different from other black girls that she knew and she often felt out of place around people of her own race. Her proper Canadian accent did not help either. Destiny moved from Canada, her birth place, to Texas when she was fourteen years old and she felt out of place ever since. Texan girls had curves and pretty faces. She, on the other hand, was pencil shaped and did not see beauty when she looked in the mirror. Destiny had always been a tomboy and viewed herself as unattractive – to her, any attention was good attention. Destiny's smile was the only thing that she wore proudly, but even that was not genuine – it was a mask.

Destiny bent over and kissed her daughter on the cheek. Her daughter pranced off to join the rest of her classmates. Little man, her son, was in the infant room and had one teacher who tended only to him. She handed the caretaker his medicine for the day and placed her hand on her son's face, cupping his cheek in her palm. She took a deep breath, and left. It was confirmation. Her mind was made up.

The little silver car parked in the dirt filled driveway stood out like a sore thumb. It was always so clean and sparkly, like it was fresh off the lot. It was out of place though, as the scenery behind it was unpleasant. Destiny always hated coming over here. There was always a stench in the air, like this neighborhood had gotten an extra dose of pollution – a little more than the rest of the world. There were stray dogs everywhere searching for food and clean water, while fleas were having a fiesta on their mangy backs. I did not like coming over here either – I was not welcomed, but my reasons were far different.

"There goes my girl." He came from behind the driver's seat of the silver trophy parked in front of the pale yellow house and welcomed her with a warm hug. The beads hanging from his neatly braided hair fell gently onto her shoulders. His cigarette scented breath gently warmed her neck and the new growth of his beard lightly pricked her cheeks as they stood in a thirty second embrace. That was usually how long it lasted. To her though, it seemed to have lasted for hours. She melted every time. His arms made her feel so safe and she forgot about every problem. To her, he was flawless. No one had ever held her like that, and he knew it.

He walked her through the side door, which barely held on to its hinges, through the roach infested kitchen, and down a dark hallway. The smell of mold and cigarettes teased her nostrils, but she held her breath every time. They got to a room lit with black lights and candles. The room was not even ten feet from the entrance, but it felt like miles away to her. She quickly shut the door behind her and exhaled.

"Really? Is it that bad?" he laughed, lighting a cigarette.

"Bad isn't the word Eric. It stinks! This house, if that's what you call it, is filthy and I can't wait until you get another studio, if you ever do."

Eric aka Epic, the Charming, had been using the little room in the back, free of charge, and converted it into his studio. He was a locally recognized singer and producer. The house belonged to the mother of two members of his entourage, or "friends" as they called themselves. Epic was Chief of the self-made organization, and they were nothing more than his puppets. He had charisma and a gift of gab that was not only persuasive, but addictive. He verbalized whatever he had to say with an authoritative tone. He was a chameleon, able to take any situation and make it his own. He could be a smart and savvy businessman, or a hard and intimidating street mogul. He had the look, he had the style, and he had the ambition to satisfy his greed. He was a master manipulator and disguised it with pride and status. *He* was Charming.

"First of all, you know better than to call me by my real name" he said, raising his cigarette in the air.

Destiny rolled her eyes playfully, "Sorry … Epic"

"Thank you." The Charming smiled. "Secondly, this is why we need to get a head start on our business."

She looked around and nodded her head in agreement. The studio was the only thing in the house that didn't smell like cheesy feet and musk, and it was like the roaches invading the rest of the house knew better than to enter this room. But the room was tiny and got easily overcrowded.

"…and the sooner the better" he continued. He loved to hear himself talk – especially since everything he said was always right, according to him.

"Sooner? Like how much sooner?" Destiny asked with her eyebrows raised.

"Like 'this weekend' sooner" he grinned.

I wanted so badly to shield her ears from this nonsense, but I could not intervene, not until I received the command. It was required that she be tested first. She had to make this decision on her own.

"Are you kidding me? That's three days away. I have to get my kids together and, and everything!"

Epic reached into his pocket and pulled out a wad of money.

"Only for two weeks. We'll go get settled, and then come back. We'll plan for the three months" he said as he handed her the money.

"You want me to leave for Dallas in three days? Impossible!"

"Just ask one of those best friends you're always talking about to watch your kids for a of couple weeks. That's more than enough money to pay them and get the kiddos what they need. Money talks."

She sighed, as she put the money in her purse. "Two weeks."

Destiny was hesitant. If she had thought about it any longer she would have changed her mind, and he was well aware of that.

I bowed my head in disappointment as I stood back and watched Destiny dive into a pool of disaster. Oh how I wanted to save her, but the test was required. I was not in fear of her drowning, for I knew that was not authorized. Even so, it was painful to see her head sink below the water. The test – she was failing. But it was not over. It was far from over.

He sang in the most beautiful voice as he stoked her chin, "Don't worry baby, everything will be okay. Just believe and trust… in me." I found that voice to be annoying and tone deafening, but she loved it.

He continued to marvel her in song, hitting notes that only he could hit. No one else in his group could sing like him, which is how he gained his status in the first place.

He was raised in a good home and had a good childhood, but he got a taste of lust and fame at an early age. At age eleven he was recognized by a famous Houston rapper for his superb vocal ability and was contracted to sing background vocals on his album. Ever since then, power, fame, and money were all he hungered for. By the time he left the record label at age seventeen, he was well known and had been through more money than the average teen.

When his parents saw that he was spiraling out of control they tried to put an end to it, but that did not stop Eric. He left home, had an older female get him his own apartment, and pursued his own record label. He created an alter ego, Epic, which would become his street name because he believed that his poetic lyrics were food to the soul. He viewed himself as a hero to women, rescuing their image, because when one was with him, they mattered. Since he had worked with such a famous artist, he attracted women of all ages. They would buy him clothes, get him credit cards, cars, and, most of all, enable his ego. He turned into a full-blown womanizer. Epic developed the philosophy that if he could not use them, then he did not need them. He believed that women were his key to anything and used them for anything – no exceptions. Sadly, Destiny was magnetized to his charm and was no exception either.

"I'll be here for you, always," he continued to sing.

She smiled, and again her heart melted as he sang into her soul. Deep into her soul. Still singing, he turned and began flicking buttons on his equipment. He had her convinced that her very presence inspired him to make great music. He wanted her to stay while he worked, and Destiny did not mind it one bit. She enjoyed every moment with him – her ears tickled by the sweet melodies he created. She would indulge in his companionship all day if she could.

A couple of hours passed and it was time for Destiny to return to reality. Once again, her romantic voyage had ended for the day and she would take with her only the notes imprinted on her heart. She stood up from the black leather couch in the corner of the room and headed towards the door. He grabbed her from behind with both hands tightly positioned around her tiny waist. She felt his lips behind her ear. Chills went down her spine and she could feel the hairs on the back of her neck stand up.

"Trust me, this trip will be worth it. Just trust me," he whispered.

He sealed the deal with a warm, passionate peck on the side of her neck, right under her ear. That was all it took – a single peck. It wasn't even a full kiss. Her mind was made up. Destiny held her breath as she walked down the filthy hallway, back into the pest-infested kitchen. The lady of the house, the mother of the two men in Epic's clique whom the house belonged, was cooking. The lazy dog that always followed behind her was asleep at her feet. Destiny tried to sneak passed her and almost made it to the side door that was hanging off of its hinges.

"Hey there slim!" the lady said, with her curly gray hair and large cooking spoon in hand.

"Oh hi Miss Terry. How are you?"

"I'm fine sweetie. Sneaking off so soon?"

"Yes ma'am," Destiny said trying to inch towards the door. "I have to go pick up my babies."

"Oh good. How are those babies anyway?"

"They are just fine Miss…."

"I remember when my boys were babies" Miss Terry interrupted. "Yep, they used to be some good boys. I don't know what done happened nowadays though. Ever since they started hanging with… him!"

Miss Terry pointed the spoon, dripping with some sort of gravy, towards the little door of the studio. A drop of the sauce hit the floor. Destiny had been warned about Miss Terry. She was told that she had gone crazy since her husband died years ago, and it had recently gotten worse. Destiny could tell. The old lady was always babbling and complaining about something. She always thought that people were out to get her and everyone else, including Destiny. This time, she was right.

She rambled on. "Slim," she called Destiny, "you're a sweet girl. Watch your back, because he's going to take you down."

"Why do you say that Miss Terry?"

"He did it to me and my boys. Said all he needed was six months to make some money, now he run my house! Been that way for over a year now. I see all kinds of evil come from that there room! All kinds of evil." A greasy grey curl broke loose from one of the rollers in her hair and covered her left eye as she squinted and her voice got raspy.

Destiny moved a step closer to the door.

"Hmm-hmm" she continued, "My boys used to be good boys. Now I see all kinds of evil in them too." Her voice got raspier and now she was almost whispering. "All kinds of evil" she repeated.

Destiny stood there puzzled, trying to figure out the old lady. What made her so paranoid?

"Miss T, you in there talking crazy again?" Epic yelled entering the kitchen.

"What you talking 'bout boy?" Miss Terry was startled. Destiny hadn't heard the studio door open either.

The dog by the old lady's foot popped his head up. His eyes struggled to see passed the bush of hair that covered his face – he was long overdue for a grooming. His tan colored fur had started to tangle and looked like honey-blonde dread locks. He tilted his head to the side as he stared at Epic, examining his every word.

"I'm talking about whatever you're talking about" Epic teased sarcastically, preying on the old lady's dementia.

"I'm just offering the child some food. You want some chicken and dumplings baby?"

Destiny looked at the muck that surrounded the pot of food bubbling on the stove. The old lady still held the spoon in her hand, which was now dripping the slimy substance all over the floor.

"Umm, no ma'am I'll be late, but thank you." Destiny felt nausea attacking her stomach and turned towards the door.

"Ok baby. You take care now and be careful, hear?" The old lady raised her silver-colored brows at Destiny as though they had shared a secret.

Epic grabbed Destiny by her hand and escorted her outside.

"Don't mind her, she's nuts!" Epic kicked a couple of rocks out of the way to clear the path for Destiny.

"Yeah, you've told me that before. But it's so sad."

Epic shrugged his shoulders. "Life" he grunted.

He didn't care to discuss much that did not involve him or money. Destiny, on the other hand, was different. She had a heart for everyone – even for him. He walked her to her car and kissed her forehead.

"I have to go pick up my baby" he yelled out of the window as he lit another cigarette.

"Okay" Destiny smiled as she put her car in reverse.

He blew her a kiss, and drove away.

Destiny was happy that he was so interactive with his children, and of how highly he spoke of them. He had two daughters, from different women, but played a big part in both of their lives. It was unusual for parents to get along unless they were in a relationship, so Destiny was impressed that he and the children's mothers were able to be civil.

Destiny had met the mother of the newborn a while back at a popular lounge in downtown Houston, where Epic was performing, and she seemed pretty cool. The two ladies did not get a chance to converse, but Epic did introduce them. He introduced his child's mother, Spirit, as a fellow artist, and introduced Destiny as a supporter of his music. At the time that they met Destiny wasn't involved with Epic. Coincidentally, Destiny had met Epic through a former friend of hers, who was involved with him at that time, named Vision.

Vision, like Epic, was also a vocal artist. The two met in the summer of 2000 at a music event hosted in Houston. I remember that day so vividly. Vision received an invitation to perform at the event that would be broadcasted on live television, and she wanted all of her close friends to be there. Destiny was supposed to accompany her that very day, but she had to work late and was unable to attend, so Vision invited two other friends to join her – the twins. The girls frequently did things together and were known for always being in their group of four. But that day, there were only three. Destiny was not there – she was not supposed to be. She was never supposed to be. However, the day came when Vision introduced Destiny to the guy band and it was not long before the two groups became close. Too close. They meshed into one big crew and started doing everything together, fun things. At least that was what everyone thought; everyone but Epic. To him, no time should be wasted, and with every minute, there was motive. He always had a motive.

Vision, like Destiny, was raised in the church and had a strong spiritual foundation. Her parents were always active in the church, and her mother was a powerful prayer warrior. Though she too was misguided and often derailed from her true calling, she always found her way back to her foundation. Vision was outspoken and strong-minded, and had always been that way. She and Destiny met at Faith Tabernacle in 1994, when Destiny moved to Texas, and had been friends ever since.

Vision was the one person that Destiny secretly admired and looked up to. She was beautiful, had a strong personality, and was super talented. Destiny would get chills whenever Vision shared her beautiful gift of song. She could walk into a quiet room full of people and turn the silence into smiles and laughter. Destiny truly loved her like a sister – she was the glue of the small group of friends, and Epic knew it. He observed the girls closely for months and identified the weak from the strong. It was then that he put his plan into action – to divide and conquer.

Epic became intimate with Vision and started belittling Destiny and the twin sisters. He would talk badly behind Destiny and the other girls' backs, asking Vision why she was even friends with them. He made jokes about "turning the girls out – especially that skinny one!" referring to Destiny. Vision never took Epic seriously, and in fear of hurting her friends, she kept quiet about the comments.

Over time, Vision decided to work things out with her boyfriend, whom she had been hiding her secret life with Epic from. It was like one day something just clicked, and she no longer wanted to be associated with Epic and his crew, *her crew*. She saw the red flags, heard the silent alarms, felt disaster brewing ahead, and she left. Quietly and quickly she left, hoping that her friends would follow, but they didn't. They did not hear or see the danger that Vision did, so they stayed. Destiny stayed.

Vision was no longer intertwined with the "group". She had broken free from the poisonous web of lust that was getting stronger and stronger each day. Vision was out of the picture. It was then that Epic, The Charming, began to pursue his plan. Destiny was his plan, and Destiny had fallen for it. Completely magnetized to his charm, she had become delusional. Destiny had no regard for how Vision would feel. She had drowned in a fallacy of enchantment, which she had dreamed of her whole life. Finally, someone would love her and say so. Finally, someone would hold her and she feel it. Finally someone would make her feel like a prize – like she existed. She longed for the fatherly-type love that she was deprived of growing up. Finally, someone would look deep into her eyes and tell her that she was beautiful. Blinded by emotion, deafened by her insecurities, and in disregard of the cost, she was in love – in love with being loved. Unaware of the comments that he made behind her back, and unaware of his motives, Destiny opened her heart to the very person whose intentions were to destroy it. She had become vulnerably transparent.

3

THE SIGNS

Clothes filled the little twin bed as Destiny anxiously scrambled through them. Her son napped in the car seat at the foot of the bed and she could hear her daughter at the dinner table in the kitchen, engaged in a deep conversation with her roommate's father. Destiny called him dad, and her children knew him as Pa-Pa. The house was a comfortable size: three bedrooms, two bathrooms, and a big back yard. It was always filled with family, friends, and just random visitors that would stop by to chat with Dad – he was a very wise man and loved by the community. There was no room for a mother and two children, in addition to the family of three which already resided there.

Destiny was only supposed to be living in the home with her friend's family temporarily, after the last falling out that she had with her mother. She had left her mother's home several times before due to major disagreements, and promised that this would be the last move. She was determined to get on her own two feet and refused to return to her mother's home. Her mind was made up.

The family she was living with was very warm and made her feel at home, but there was something, perhaps another insecurity, telling her that time was up for her and her children. Destiny felt they had exhausted their welcome. It was time to leave. I agreed it was time for her to leave that house, but not like this.

"So what's up?" the roommate plopped on the bed opposite of Destiny's. "What is all this? And what do you have to tell me?" she asked curiously.

The roommate, Tiffany, was one of Destiny's close friends and a part of the small girl circle that Vision had abandoned. They met as neighbors in the same apartment complex in 1999. The chemistry was almost instant and Tiffany and Destiny quickly became inseparable. Tiffany had a twin sister named Tina, but the two had completely different personalities. The twins were originally from Waco, Texas, but came to join their father in Houston for a taste of the city life, and they loved it. Destiny not only bonded with the girls, but also adopted their father as her own and he played the role remarkably.

"Come on, tell me!" Tiffany demanded.

Destiny moved her sleeping son closer to her and shut the door. "Are you ready for this?" she teased.

"Just tell me already! I've been waiting all day!"

Destiny put the pink shirt she had been fumbling with on top of the pile of clothes on the bed. She took a deep breath, and sat next to the pile. "O…k…" Destiny began.

Tiffany put her hands on her forehead, rubbing the wrinkles that had surfaced from her expression of disbelief. They soon moved to cover her eyes, and then her mouth as she listened to the details of Destiny's new 'job'. She nervously fondled the long fizzy ponytail that overlapped her shoulder as Destiny continued.

"Well? What do you think?" Destiny asked cautiously awaiting her friend's opinion.

"What about the kids?"

Destiny got up and went towards her purse hanging on the closet door. She pulled out the wad of money which had been untouched. Tiffany's eyes lit up.

"I just need you to watch them for two weeks." Destiny began to loosen the wad. "I already asked my cousin about the three months and she said yes. But that's not until a few months from now."

Destiny handed her roommate a small stash folded together. "It's six hundred exactly. That should be good for two weeks, right?"

"What?" Tiffany snatched the stash out of Destiny's hand in shock. "Oh my goodness, you're serious!"

Destiny paused. "Am I serious?" she thought to herself. She glanced down at her baby boy nestled in his car seat. She nodded her head – she was serious.

The roommate placed the hundred dollar bills on her bed and stood up to face Destiny. "I got your back. Just be careful" she said to Destiny.

Destiny could feel her eyes filling with tears. Why was she so emotional? It was just a job. In a way, she wanted her friend to tell her how silly she was and that she should not go on this 'business trip'. She wanted her friend to tell her that she would never speak to her again if she went. But she didn't. Instead, Tiffany encouraged her, enabling her to depend on the twisted fantasy she had created with The Charming. For a moment, Destiny subconsciously heard the voice of Vision and even thought about calling her. She knew if anyone would talk her out of such foolishness it would be Vision; but the moment passed more quickly than it came, replacing itself with guilt. Her former friend would never answer the phone anyway. No one was there to reveal the danger that was hidden in the fine print of the deal. I tried, but she couldn't hear me. It was official – she was going.

Destiny spent the rest of the week preparing for her vocational adventure. She contacted all of her son's therapists and made arrangements around her roommate's schedule, prepaid the children's daycare, and refilled medication. She bought them brand new clothes, toys, and books, which she had to hide in the closet. She told the temporary agency that she wouldn't need any job placement for the next two weeks. With the help of the roommate, Destiny came up with a convincing story to tell Dad, because he would never approve of her leaving her kids for so long. They told him that Destiny was hired by a client of the temporary agency where she worked and was being sent out of town for training.

"Training" he repeated peculiarly as he listened carefully to the girls' story.

"Yes" the roommate squealed, trying to assure her father.

They told him about a company located in Dallas that they researched on the Internet and even found a job description for one of the positions the company had so that they could provide facts to support their story. The story was believable. He couldn't argue with facts, and he couldn't justify his feelings. He knew something was wrong, but his instincts were not enough to argue against their lies.

"Okay" he said grudgingly. "Call every day and be careful."

He put his head back down in the newspaper spread across his lap, fighting the tugging he felt inside. He sighed. "Okay" he repeated to himself. The ladies gave each other a swift wink of victory. They couldn't believe that their story had actually worked. He was usually a hard one to pull the wool over, but they did it. Destiny did it. Though deep inside, she wished he too would have forbidden her plan. Oh well. That was the last obstacle. It was her last escape. She was going.

It was finally Friday. Destiny moaned at the alarm screaming in her ear. Her roommate pressed her headphones against her ears. Destiny reached to the nightstand and hit the small black clock. The blinking red numbers appeared blurry. She yawned and stretched at the same time, her arms extended above her head. Then the thought came to her – it was Friday. This was it. She jumped out of the bed and darted to bathroom.

"This is it," she whispered to herself, staring into the square mirror above the sink. It felt like graduation day or a wedding day. It felt like she was about to walk down an aisle that would change her life forever. Indeed, it would. Destiny didn't bother sending her two children to daycare that day. Instead, she took them to the Houston Zoo, then to the little park beside the zoo, and then to see Shrek for the second time! Destiny would have seen the kiddie movie a dozen more times if that's what it took to spend each moment with her children. The entire day was spent with her two little angels. Oddly, though, this day seemed shorter than the others. The day was almost over, and the time was near.

"Buckle up!" Destiny sang, looking to her daughter through her rear-view mirror.

"Yes ma'am" she sang back.

It was already six o'clock. Destiny and the children had been out all day, but she couldn't believe how fast the time had passed.

She had so much fun with them and wished she could freeze the digital clock in her car, which now read 6:11 pm.

"Mommy," a sweet voice came from the back seat of the car.

"Yes baby?" "Are you leaving?" the little girl asked.

"Only to get presents, angel. I'll be back very soon."

The little girl was quiet for a few seconds as she contemplated her next thought. "Can I go?"

"No, baby. Only mommy can go get the presents because it has to be a surprise." Destiny tried to make it sound fun.

The little girl leaned her head on her brother's car seat and closed her eyes. The drive home was a long one – especially with all of the thoughts that clustered Destiny's mind. Would her children be okay? Would they look different in two weeks? Would they be mad at her? Would her roommate be able to handle her son and his special needs? I threw more intense thoughts her way to try and divert her decision, but every time she looked in that rear-view mirror at her two sleeping babies, she said it again, "I have to do this."

Destiny got her kids ready for bed and headed outside. Dad was putting the suitcase in the car. The street was quiet and the neighborhood kids had cleared the driveways of the small brick homes. It was a middle-class neighborhood located just fifteen minutes from Temple Church. The houses were old, and the people whom resided in them were of the older generation. It was always a quiet street, but tonight, it seemed extra quiet. Not even the sound of crickets could be heard. It was like a death-stricken silence. "Why are y'all leaving so late?" he asked, taking a puff of the cigar hanging from his mouth.

"My coworker had to work late today, and tomorrow is too late of a start. We want to get settled in early." Destiny was always a quick thinker under pressure.

He reached in his back pocket and pulled out an old brown leather wallet. He took out fifty bucks and handed it to her. "Just in case," he said.

"No, I'm fine. I just got paid." Destiny turned the money away again.

He slid the money back into his back pocket, the opposite one this time. He reached out and gave Destiny a hug. "Daughter, please be careful" he said firmly. Again he felt an inner tugging. He fought the urge to snatch the keys out of the ignition. Instead, he turned away and went in the house.

"Take care of my babies. I'll call a dozen times a day" Destiny chuckled, facing her roommate who stood beside her car speechless.

"Wow. You're really going through with this" she mumbled.

Destiny threw her purse on the passenger side of her vehicle and turned to her roommate, "I'll be okay. Promise."

She hopped into the driver's seat, fixed her mirrors, threw on a quick touch of lip gloss, and was off. *We* were off. I shadowed her closely. As she drove through the darkness I could hear whispers and hackling of the 'others', the voices of darkness. They chanted and cheered victoriously, but this battle was not over.

4

THE COUNTDOWN

At least the raggedy yellow house couldn't be seen so well at night time. There were no street lights on this street. There was a tiny, dim, porch light that hung over the front entrance of the house. Mosquitoes gathered around it as it flickered on and off. There were more cars over here tonight than usual. There were always three or four, but this time at least eight cars lined the street, condensing it to the size of an alley. By the side door where Destiny normally entered the house, was a swirl of smoke that blossomed into the air as three men stood around it. One big, one tall, and one really big. Destiny could hear them laughing and joking from her car.

The side door swung open. Destiny giggled as the three men appeared to stand to attention. That always happened when he came around. Epic stopped by the group of men and got a cigarette from one of them. He looked over, saw her car, and displayed a huge smile. She smiled back, picked up her purse, and headed towards him. He met her halfway and kissed her on her cheek, holding the cigarette away from her face. He knew she couldn't stand the smell of smoke. Every member in his entourage smoked. His brother smoked, the promoters smoked, his fans smoked – they smoked so they should have been called Smoke.

"You made it. I thought you changed your mind" he said, still smiling.

Destiny shook her head, "Nah, I thought about it though."

"Well I'm glad you didn't." He put his arm around her shoulder as they approached the group of guys standing by the door.

"Y'all know my queen" he bragged.

It broke down every self-conscious wall that she had when he talked like that. The men greeted her as such and bowed jokingly. Destiny was very familiar with two of the guys; they were Miss Terry's sons and shared the little yellow house with her.

"Oh and this is my boy." Epic pointed to the unfamiliar one, "He'll be the driver. Just call him Zee."

"The driver?" Destiny asked shockingly.

"Of course," he replied, "I told you – you won't be doing much of anything. Not even driving."

Zee extended his hand to greet Destiny with a handshake, but Epic pulled her away before she could react.

They took the journey down the dark, moldy hallway to the studio. Behind the door Destiny could hear voices that she had never heard before. Epic opened the door with one hand around her shoulder. Destiny's breath paused for about a half of a second. She was shocked to see new faces. The room was clouded with smoke and in the corner beside the black leather couch stood two half-dressed females. One was Caucasian with dyed red hair and a fake mole on her cheek, and the other was black with big hips and an extra curly weave. They huddled nervously in the corner, sharing a burnt down cigarette.

Destiny noticed another girl on the couch, but this one looked familiar. Destiny was certain that they had met before. It was obvious that she had more confidence than the other ladies. She was spread comfortably on the black leather, with one of her legs propped up on the arm of the couch. She looked at Destiny from head to foot and made circles with the smoke coming from her mouth. Her skin was golden brown and her long lashes glittered in the black light that filled the room. She rolled her eyes and ran her fingers through her long black hair as she stared at Epic, questions written all over her face. Destiny was appalled. What was this fake princess wanna-be doing in her seat anyway? Everyone knew that the black leather couch was designated for Destiny and Destiny alone.

Epic quickly pierced the tension with a shallow introduction.

"Destiny, this is the mother of my newborn." He turned to the girl on the couch still stroking her long black hair, "This is Destiny. Remember? I think y'all met before."

The girl did not respond and her facial expression didn't change one bit. Her eyes remained fixated on Destiny. Destiny remembered meeting the girl, but she was now in defense mode and didn't say a word either. Animosity had engulfed the atmosphere. Epic introduced the two stripper-like females huddled in the corner in a single breath. They held no significance. They were not the threat.

"Alright, ladies, now that we're all here we can hit the road" Epic said, happily clapping his hands together.

"We?" Destiny snapped.

"Baby," he whispered as he stood directly in front of her and grabbed both of her hands, "we need a team. I'll explain when we get there." He gave her a quick kiss on the lips. "Now let's go."

He left her standing there and disappeared into the dark hallway with three members of his entourage following behind him. The two stripper duplicates brushed passed Destiny with their heads down. Destiny could hear skin rubbing against the leather couch as the girl, the feisty one, bounced off of it. She pulled down the tight short shorts that hugged her legs, positioned herself right in front of Destiny, and arrogantly put her hand out.

"So you're Destiny, huh?"

"Yes ma'am" Destiny responded with the driest voice possible. Barely gripping the girl's finger tips, she gave her a dull handshake in response to the girl's arrogant approach.

"Well they call me Spirit. It's nice to finally meet you," the girl said sarcastically.

Destiny returned the sarcasm with a fake smile and left the room. She could feel the girl eyeing her every move.

"This should be interesting" Destiny mumbled to herself as she walked outside to meet the rest of the crowd. I too knew this would be interesting, to say the least.

Epic was already in his little silver car waiting. The entourage gathered around the tiny driveway, still smoking their cigarettes.

"Y'all be safe!" one of them yelled.

"Get back in one piece!" another shouted.

It was like they knew something Destiny did not. She could see something other than concern hidden in the grins on their faces and didn't waste any time trying to analyze them. She had a greater focus to worry about, a greater threat. Epic motioned with his hands for Destiny to get into the car with him. Destiny started towards the car and wanted so badly to get into that car so that she could interrogate him about his little fiasco. Just then she felt someone brush against her arm. It was Spirit, the feisty one, who had hurried passed Destiny and found her way in the front seat of the vehicle, right beside Epic.

"Come on babe," Epic hollered out of the window. "There's plenty of room."

Destiny rolled her eyes and fiercely headed in the direction of the car parked behind him with the two strippers and The Driver. One of the strippers was in the front seat, but as Destiny approached the brown old-school looking car, she quickly hopped to the backseat. Destiny plopped down in the passenger side and positioned her seat as far back as it would go; she was practically lying down. The girls in the back seat scooted close to the opposite side to get out of Destiny's way. Destiny was furious.

"You have bags or something?" Zee asked.

Destiny pointed to the trunk of the little silver car in front of them.

"You okay?" Zee asked, trying to make conversation.

Destiny put one hand over her forehead, covering her eyebrows. She closed her eyes and went into a zone. Questions filled her mind, anxiety flooded her chest – her heart felt like it was on fire. Zee turned the radio up, put the gear in drive, and proceeded to follow the little silver car. We were leaving. It was time.

5

THE TERRITORY

It was a long and quiet ride. Destiny had not spoken a word the entire time, and the two strippers slept most of the way. Destiny ignored the attempts of The Driver, Zee, to engage in casual conversation. The radio was his only entertainment because her lips were sealed and she wanted to talk to no one. She didn't even bother to budge at a restroom stop. Instead, she stayed in the car in her own little zone.

Zee was relieved to finally make it to their destination. It had been an awkward drive for him because of Destiny's attitude. Destiny glared out of the window, focusing her attention on the big yellow lights surrounding the hotel. Zee pulled into an empty parking space beside the little silver car he had been tailing for the four hour drive. From the side view mirror, Destiny could see Epic in the office saying something to the manager of the building. From the corner of her eye she could see Spirit in the passenger side of the silver car playing with her long black hair. Destiny felt the rage that had simmered down begin to arise within her all over again. The questions flooded her thoughts. Just then, there was a knock at the window. Destiny jumped. She looked up to see Epic holding a set of room keys in his hand with a huge smile planted on his face. Destiny sighed and opened the door, slightly pushing him out of the way. She knew her limits. She got out of the car without making any eye contact. Though their faces almost touched, she looked straight passed him as if he didn't exist.

"This one is ours," he said, pointing to the room that was at an angle from where the two cars were parked.

"Okay," she said with a nonchalant attitude.

Zee was already taking bags out of the trunk. Epic handed him one of the white plastic keys and pointed to the room upstairs. He headed up the stairs and the two strippers trailed behind him. Epic put both arms around Destiny's neck and sucked her into one of those heart melting embraces. Shockingly, it did not faze her like it usually did. She was still too upset. The passenger door of the little silver car opened and Spirit stood up, stretching her arms.

"Woo! That was a long drive," she said with a smirk on her face. Her smirk got smaller as she noticed the sparks flaring from Destiny and Epic's romantic embrace. Epic released his grip and turned to Spirit.

"You need to stay upstairs with the others tonight and get the girls settled in" he said.

Destiny watched as Spirit's face turned upside down. She saw the anger brewing in Spirit's eyes.

"Okay," Spirit responded.

She took off upstairs pretending like her feelings were not hurt, like they had not just been stomped on, chewed up, and spit out. Destiny knew better, though, because it was the same roller coaster of feelings she had experienced four hours prior. In a sense, Destiny was relieved that she would finally have an opportunity to be alone with Epic. She should have been laughing in Spirit's arrogant face, but she simply couldn't. There was something about that girl. What was it? What was this circus that Epic had enlisted her in? Suddenly Destiny found herself completely clueless. What had she gotten herself into?

Destiny didn't utter a word as she watched Epic bounce around the suite in excitement. He was full of words, as usual. He went on and on about how great his idea was. His voice went in one ear and out the other as she cuddled in the soft recliner beside the big screen television. She couldn't help but think about the drama that may have been brewing in the room above them. What were the strippers really doing here? What was their part in this *business* deal? Why did they need *a driver?* She was especially curious of the feisty one, Spirit.

Epic realized that he was conversing with himself. He huddled over the recliner where Destiny sat and put both arms around her.

"What's wrong?" he asked.

"Is he serious?" Destiny thought to herself.

"What's wrong?" she sarcastically replied.

Epic removed his arms from around her, took a seat on the couch beside the big recliner, and looked into her eyes. "She has experience in this business," he said referring to Spirit. "I had to bring her. She knows this city better than I do – she used to live out here."

"So coming here was her idea?" Destiny asked in frustration.

"No babe. It was my idea, but she's worked out here off and on since she was fifteen. She knows these streets and knows all the hotspots, all the money-making spots" he smiled.

"Well, why here? Why Dallas? Why'd we have to come on her territory? We could have stayed in Houston!"

"Well, well, well," he teased, "someone sounds jealous. Look, vice has Houston on lockdown and there is more money out here."

Destiny sighed and listened, increasingly curious about this experience he spoke of. More money? Vice? Destiny finally started piecing the puzzle together.

He continued, "It's going to make our jobs a lot easier with her here, trust me."

"So are you guys a couple?"

He burst into a hard laughter, leaning back on the love seat.

"How could I be with her if I'm with you?" he said still laughing. He placed his feet on the coffee table and picked up a remote laying on the floor. "She's a business partner," he emphasized, "and the mother of my child. That's it." He started flipping through channels and said nothing else about it.

Destiny looked around at the suite and sighed. A strange feeling began to haunt her, but she ignored it. She went into the restroom and washed her face. As the water dripped down her face, she stared into the eyes of the image in the mirror. It was an unrecognizable image. She canvassed the image and began to clothe it with an imaginary garment – a costume. One that covered every inch of her body; it hid the shame that had begun to slowly come over her. She no longer knew the person in the mirror and refused to acknowledge her existence. Destiny had become Destiny.

6

THE BOND

It was Monday. The weekend had passed, and Destiny spent most of her time on the love seat watching television and talking to her daughter on the phone. She never paid much attention to the noises coming from the flat screen, she was just grateful for the distraction. They had only been there for two days, but it already felt like weeks to Destiny, who had never been away from her children for this long. I watched as tears frequently gathered in in her eyes, but she fought them before they had a chance to surface on her face. The rest of the team, Zee, the two strippers, and Spirit, never came downstairs. Even Epic spent the majority of his time upstairs, telling Destiny only that he was getting things in order. Indeed, he was.

The door swung open, "Honey I'm home!" Epic said playfully with bags in his hands. His cheek bones sat high on his face and he carried a huge smile. Behind him was Zee and one of the strippers. Behind them was her, Spirit. She paced slowly behind the crew with a pair of large round sunglasses placed perfectly on her nose, with no smile to be found.

"Are you hungry, babe?" Epic asked Destiny, dropping the bags on the floor. He sat down beside her and laid his head on her lap.

"Not really," she replied with her eyes still fixed on the television.

"Well go get something anyway," he said, handing her the money that he had pulled out of his pocket.

"I really don't have an appetite" she insisted.

"Destiny, you haven't really eaten anything for the past two days. I don't want you getting sick on me, baby."

With his head still in Destiny's lap he removed the gold-framed glasses from his face. One of the strippers came and took them out of his hand and put them in the small green case on the counter by the kitchen. She went back over by Zee and pulled a pack of cigarettes out of the black purse strapped across her chest. Epic shook his index finger back and forth and the girl timidly put the pack of cigarettes back into her purse.

"Besides," he continued, "you and Spirit are going to take a trip to the mall anyway."

Destiny looked down on her lap. His eyes were closed, but he was still talking. "You guys need to go get some new clothes" he finished.

"I brought enough clothes with me" Destiny said, puzzled.

Epic gave her a partial smile, eyes still closed. He lifted his head at an angle, giving her just enough room to slide out from under him. Destiny sat there for a second and took a deep breath. She put her shoes on and bolted out the door. Spirit turned and followed behind her, dangling the keys in her hand. Destiny went around to the passenger side of the little silver car and waited for Spirit to unlock the door, but Spirit took her sweet time, lighted a cigarette first, and then flicked the locks.

"Thank you!" Destiny said rudely. She slammed the door and immediately assumed her position to face towards the window. Spirit said nothing. The mall was about thirty minutes away and the two ladies did not utter a word to each other the entire time. They submitted to the hypnotic oath of Epic and refused to break the spell of trust that he controlled them with. They each believed two different sequels of his theatrical production: They were the stars, but only he knew the script.

Spirit made a screeching turn pulling into the driveway of the mall. She crept around the busy parking lot until she found an empty spot. She put the car in park, pulled down the mirror above her head, and dug into her purse until she found a small tube of pink lip gloss. She applied a smooth layer to her lips and then slid the sunglasses perched on her head over her eyes. The air conditioner was blowing full force and her silky black hair danced in its breeze. Destiny unbuckled her seatbelt and unlocked her door.

"Hold up" Spirit said with her hand up.

Destiny froze with her back facing Sprit. She rolled her eyes and sat there awaiting a confrontation.

"What's the deal with you?" Spirit asked. She removed the shades that covered her eyes and slid them back on top of her head.

"What's the deal with you?" Destiny snapped back.

"No, I'm serious. Please tell me what's really going on."

Spirit's tone had changed. Destiny could hear the genuine curiosity in her voice and turned towards Spirit. The attitude Spirit wore had left. Destiny saw something in her and found herself empathizing with her.

"I don't know," Destiny sighed, shrugging her shoulders.

Spirit put her head down and poked out her glossy lips like she was trying to catch the tear that had fallen from one of her eyes.

"Look," Destiny began to explain, "all I know is that he said you were here with us because you were an expert. I'm not quite sure what that means."

Spirit sniffled, "With us?"

Destiny nodded her head, "Yeah."

"He told me that you were the one here with us."

"What?" Destiny asked, afraid of what she would hear next.

"Yeah, he said that you were here because you wanted to help us."

Destiny could feel her heartbeat banging against her chest. There was a golf ball sized lump stuck in her throat and butterflies fluttered in her stomach. "Wow," she hesitantly mumbled.

"So, you guys are a couple?" Spirit asked under her breath.

Destiny could only nod.

"So are we" Spirit whispered.

The two girls sat in the car in silence for almost five minutes. They had been played – Destiny had been played. She could finally see it. But even then, she was unaware of the dangerous game she had signed up for. She was drowned in a sea of false emotions, and it was too late to save herself.

"This isn't the first time you know," Spirit sobbed, "he's been doing this to me for years. I just thought since we have a baby now, it would be different."

"Years?" Destiny thought to herself.

She couldn't even formulate the words to ask for details. It was pointless. Destiny had ignored every warning sign that had come her way. She ignored the intuition of her inner discernment that told her something was wrong. This was her fault, not his. Spirit confirmed that Epic had been scum for years. He wasn't the one that had changed, Destiny was, and she was too blind to see it. Destiny was always good at blaming herself and this was the perfect opportunity to do so. She remembered how many clues she chose to ignore that should have made her realize that he was up to no good. How could she have fallen for such deceit? As Spirit revealed details about her and Epic's relationship, Destiny went numb. Spirit told her that Epic always spoke of Destiny as a friend and future business partner.

"He called you his investment," Spirit revealed.

Destiny did not bother to tell Spirit how badly Epic disrespected her during intimate conversations they had together. What was the point of telling her how he referred to her as "crazy," or how he blamed her for their failed relationship? What was the point? The damage was already done. Destiny did not have the strength to dwell on his narcissistic behavior.

"Wow," Spirit laughed, wiping the tears from her eyes. "So my boyfriend tricked me into taking a trip with him and his girlfriend," she kept laughing. She turned to Destiny and put one hand on her shoulder. "Well chick," she stated, "either we're super naïve or he is super genius."

Destiny cracked a fake smile at Spirit's lousy attempt of a joke. Destiny couldn't find the humor at all. Suddenly, it dawned on her. Destiny was out in the middle of nowhere with no vehicle, four hours away from home, no money, and without any friends or family. Her children were not with her, Dad was not with her, Tiffany was not with her, and Vision... Vision was no longer with her. It wasn't until then that she realized how much control Epic had over her. He paid her cell phone bill, bought her food – he did everything for her. She was hundreds of miles away from home with total strangers, and was completely dependent on someone who found pleasure in lying to her.

"I guess I am as crazy as he says I am," Spirit said.

Destiny did not respond. She didn't want to attend Spirit's pity party because she was too busy sulking in her own. Spirit ignored Destiny's silence and kept talking, "I know he told you."

"Told me what?" Destiny asked as she watched pedestrians walk in and out of the mall.

"About my nervous breakdown. He always uses it against me."

Destiny recalled Epic's mention of the episode, but didn't admit it. "Nope," she replied.

"Well, I'm sure he'll use it to try and cover up this mess, so I might as well tell you myself."

Destiny anxiously rubbed her thighs. Her jeans were starting to stick to her skin and she wanted nothing more than to get out of the car, and out of the conversation. Spirit ignored Destiny's body language and kept on talking. She told Destiny about her history of mental breakdowns stemming from her mother's death five years prior. Spirit had become comfortable with Destiny as she shared dark descriptions of her past. She told her how she had been molested ever since she was a toddler, and how her uncle introduced her to prostitution at the age of ten.

"My momma was clueless about what was going on, but she was all I had," she vented. "When she died, I had to take care of myself."

Spirit was crying again and black eyeliner rolled down her cheeks. She disclosed to Destiny how her mother died of Acquired Immune Deficiency Syndrome, contracted by a cheating boyfriend. Destiny was overwhelmed with everything that Spirit had told her within a span of thirty minutes. Destiny pulled a sheet of Kleenex from a pack she had in her purse and handed it to Spirit. She felt horrible for the girl. Spirit took the Kleenex and dabbed her cheeks.

"I'm sorry," Spirit apologized, "it's just that every man I've ever known has let me down. I just thought he was different, you know."

"You can't let him break you down like this," Destiny replied. "This is not your ending. Your story goes on beyond him, and I'm sure it's a happy ending" she smiled.

If only Destiny was able to hear her own words, but she didn't. She felt sympathy for Spirit. This was no longer about her. She had completely abandoned her own feelings and was immediately drawn to the heart of this stranger. "How could he do this to her?" she thought to herself. No one deserved to be treated like that. Destiny excluded herself of that thought. She felt terrible after listening to Spirit's shocking life story. Destiny paid no attention to how quickly the two had connected. She didn't question why Spirit was so transparent with her, or why she trusted Destiny enough to share her story. None of that mattered. Their souls tied together as they felt the pain pounding on each other's hearts. Destiny reached over and gave Spirit a friendly hug.

"It's going to be okay girl. You'll get through this," she whispered to Spirit.

"*We'll* get through this," Spirit repeated.

The phone buzzed loudly as it vibrated vigorously on the dashboard, interrupting the ladies sympathetic hug.

"It's him," Spirit said with her famous eye roll.

She answered the phone, mocking every word that came out of Epic's mouth. She hung up and threw the phone into her bright purple purse.

"What'd he say?" Destiny asked, looking at her phone, which was receiving a text message.

"Girl, something about a white t-shirt," she said nonchalantly.

Destiny held up her phone and showed Spirit the text message. It was from Epic telling her the exact same thing. The two ladies got out of the car and brushed the wrinkles from their outfits.

Their dramatic tear-filled union had lasted almost an hour in the little silver car.

"I know you're green, so I'll help you make it through these next couple of weeks," Spirit blurted to Destiny who was standing on the opposite side of the car.

Destiny nodded, "Okay."

She was aware that her job description had changed. She now knew the real details of the 'business deal,' and she had to do whatever it took to survive.

Destiny and Spirit agreed to keep their little conversation a secret. They had gained a small portion of Epic's control and had to protect it from him. Destiny promised Spirit that she wouldn't say a word about the abuse she endured in the past, nor speak to Epic about the history of her psychotic breakdowns. The two girls had quickly become friends and were no longer hypnotized. Instead, they pulled themselves into their own delusional trance and believed it would protect them.

Destiny had attained a new sense of responsibility. She couldn't let Spirit suffer another breakdown from another preying man. She had to help her through this. I watched closely as this unusual bond transpired between the two ladies. This was not a bond that was supposed to be made. I observed the one named Spirit closely. She was named appropriately. I felt the deceit in every breath she took and saw the spirits that invaded her soul. Spirit, indeed. I spoke clearly to myself, "Cor, prepare!" for I knew the time was near.

"What ever happened to the chick with the mole on her cheek? Wasn't there two of them?" Destiny asked as the two started towards the mall.

"She left."

"She went back to Houston? I wish I would have known, I would have hitched a ride."

"Nope," Spirit said, "not Houston."

Destiny did not bother to ask any other questions.

"She didn't make it. But you will, you're a fighter" Spirit smiled at Destiny.

Destiny returned the smile and the two new-found friends entered the mall.

7

THE MASK

It was Thursday. Almost a week had passed and Epic had held up his end of the bargain by limiting Destiny's responsibilities. Destiny saw girls come in and out of the two suites, and quite a few men as well. Destiny kept a head count of all the visitors and interviewed every client. She wore the imaginary mask that had molded to her face day and night. She didn't even take it off when she went to sleep. The majority of the clients visited the upstairs suite. Epic said that the lower room was their personal suite and didn't want too much traffic in there.

Destiny observed as she watched the man who once melted her heart turn into an emotionless monster full of greed. She too had turned into something; she felt it, but straightened her invisible mask and invisible costume and kept on playing her part. All she wanted to do was survive these two weeks and make it back home to her children.

There was no telling what Epic would do if he gained knowledge of her plan. He was always gentle toward her and had never harmed a hair on her head, but his possessive personality had grown stronger and stronger. Destiny did not know the man who salivated at the sight of money and smacked pretty faces around to get it. She stayed hidden in her invisible costume and counted down the days until she would hold her children again.

Destiny and Spirit had joined forces and together had assumed their role in the greed-infested organization. Together, they would help him reach his goal. The sooner he reached his goal, the sooner they would go home. Epic was so caught up in his fictional character of 'The Man' that he did not notice how close the two ladies had become. He did not realize that they were on to him. At that point, he would not have cared anyway. The two ladies spent all of their time together sharing stories of their past; Spirit did most of the talking. They went on shopping sprees together and lavished in the luxury of currency, accumulated by lust.

Destiny and Spirit stood in the small kitchen of the studio, cooking. One was stirring the pot of sauce for the spaghetti, and the other was tossing a salad in a small wooden bowl. The two laughed and joked as they prepared their meal.

"I'm glad to see you two are having so much fun," Epic said, bursting through the front door.

"Hey babe," the two responded at the same time, followed by a chuckle.

Epic passively ignored the joke.

"We need to talk," he said, placing the gold framed glasses on the counter.

Destiny lowered the temperature on the stove and Spirit placed the little wooden bowl in the refrigerator. The two waited for him to continue, but Destiny already knew it would be something she didn't want to hear and tried to mute his voice in her mind.

"Money isn't coming in fast enough. We're still a few grand away from our goal."

"We?" Destiny thought. There he went again with the 'we' word, knowing good and well that his plans were solo.

He went on to say that his 'employees' weren't doing so well and that they needed to be replaced. The two girls listened. Destiny watched as Spirit's facial expressions began to change. She could see her struggling on the inside as she tried to fight the words that were coming from Epic's mouth – it was like she had been down this road before. The more he spoke, the more Spirit's attitude changed.

"What do you want us to do?" Destiny interrupted.

"I need you out there with them. Guide them in the right direction."

A nervous chill spread throughout Destiny's body. She bit down on her tongue so hard that it drew blood. She feared that this would happen. She knew that one day he would renege on his promise, she just hoped to make it the whole two weeks without him doing so. She planned on telling him then that it was over and that she would not be back for another three months. She planned to tell him to take his business proposal and shove it. She planned on telling him all of this, at home, where she was safe.

Destiny cringed as Epic rambled on about Destiny's new responsibilities. Destiny and Spirit made frequent eye contact during his rampage, secretly trying to console each other's pain. Destiny knew that not even the mask that she wore would be able to hide from such horror. I looked up and revamped my strength – I was going to need it.

"Be ready by ten" Epic ended. He went into the main bedroom of the suite and laid face first across the bed. The two girls glanced at the time blinking from the microwave in the kitchen. It was 8:23 pm, and counting. They had less than two hours to get ready. Sprit walked out of the kitchen, through the back bedroom, and into the closet. Destiny followed behind her. Spirit pulled out a huge red suitcase and began to pull clothes from it.

"I guess I'll wear black tonight," she said.

Destiny could tell that Spirit wanted to burst into tears as she frantically went through the suitcase.

"Spirit," Destiny called.

Spirit kept throwing clothes all over the bed, ignoring Destiny.

"Spirit!" Destiny said again.

"What?" Spirit shouted.

Destiny reached over and shut the bedroom door. "Are you okay?" she asked, not knowing what else to say.

"I'm used to it," Spirit snapped, "this is what I do. This is me."

Destiny watched as Spirit continued chunking clothes from one end of the bed to the other. It was though she had turned into a completely different person. Destiny left the room, worried that she would upset Spirit even more. She knew she was hurt – she saw it in her eyes and felt it in her presence. The last thing Destiny wanted to do was trigger one of the episodes Spirit had told her about.

Destiny went into the bedroom where Epic was lounged on the queen-sized bed. She looked at him as he slept peacefully. How could he find so much peace in such an environment? As he slept in such a sweet slumber, Destiny could feel the atmosphere brewing, as if she was in the path of a vicious tornado. She was right. The atmosphere brewed. I prepared. Destiny walked passed the bed and reached for the tan leather suitcase propped up against the wall. She quietly removed a concoction of fiber stitched together into a scanty black and white outfit. Destiny got dressed as butterflies pranced around in her gut. The jitters were so bad that they felt like June bugs crashing into the inner lining of her stomach, and she could not shake the feeling. Destiny met Sprit in the restroom – she was concealing her sorrow with mascara and blush.

"Can you do mine too?" Destiny asked as she watched Spirit cover every detail of her face.

Without words, Spirit turned and began applying liquid foundation to Destiny's face. Destiny began to feel more at ease as Spirit piled the gunk onto her smooth skin, but the jitters were still kicking in her stomach.

"There," Spirit said adding the last touch of lipstick to Destiny's lips.

"Thanks," Destiny replied and proceeded towards the living room.

"You're not going to look at it?" Spirit asked as Destiny slumped in the seat of the recliner.

"Nope."

Destiny did not want any encounters with mirrors or any other object that would cause her to see her reflection. She knew she would not like what she saw. The person in the mirror had become a stranger, someone Destiny was now afraid of. She went into a dark, silent zone as the television began watching her. She forced every thought connected to her emotions out of her head. She blocked the voices of her conscience and tried to mute the sound of her heartbeat. Destiny felt protected in this zone, believing that if she forced her feelings away, it would not matter if they got hurt. She felt protected from Epic, protected from the evil that she would soon come to face, and protected from herself. Spirit joined her, assuming her position on the couch. The two stared into the box blankly, their thoughts distant, as sorrow began to hover over them.

Thirty minutes had passed and the short hand of the clock ticked closer to ten, as the long hand gradually approached the twelve. It was time. The girls could hear Epic in the restroom washing his face. He made a quick phone call and then entered the room where the two girls drooped hopelessly in their seats.

"You two ready?" he asked rubbing his hands together.

"Of course," Spirit said, pretending to be enthused.

Destiny followed Spirit's lead and stood to her feet. She grabbed her purse and headed towards the door. She felt a hand grab her on side. Epic lightly pinched her waist and whispered, "Just tonight."

Destiny had programmed her ears to reject the lies that flowed so smoothly out of Epic's mouth. She forced him a weak smile and continued out the door. Though something inside of her heart still felt a ruthless connection to him, her mind was aware that Epic had suckered her into a whirlwind, and her only mission now was to get out of it.

Destiny approached the brown old-school car where Spirit slumped in the back seat with her face turned towards the window. Beside her were two new faces, one young and one a little older. Zee opened the door for Destiny and the two new faces scooted over to make room. Spirit continued glaring out of the window as Zee closed the door for Destiny and went to the driver's seat of the car; Epic had already made himself comfortable in the passenger seat. The two new faces didn't appear nervous at all; they seemed familiar with the routine. Destiny, however, could now feel her heart beating in her throat. It blocked her airway and she struggled to breathe. Gasping for air, Destiny rolled her window down midway. The young new face grabbed the hair that flew in her eyes.

"Sorry," Destiny said fanning her face.

"It's okay," The young new face responded. "It is kind of stuffy in here."

Spirit glanced over at Destiny and smiled. She could see the panic in Destiny's eyes. "We're all going to stay together," Spirit belted aloud, "there's no point in us splitting up when I'm the only one that knows where to go, or what to do at all for that matter."

The older new face fixed her mouth to disagree, but Spirit instantly blocked her thoughts with a vicious stare. The older new face cowardly put her head down.

"No!" Epic responded in an authoritative voice. "You're going to split up in two's. It will be faster that way."

"That makes no sense. I know these streets like the back of my hand. It would be much faster if…"

"NO!" Epic yelled, "You're lucky I don't make you all go solo. I'm being nice!"

He had turned around in his seat to face the argumentative Spirit threatening her with his eyes.

"Don't get it twisted," he continued. "Just because you know the game doesn't mean that you run it. This is my show."

Epic turned back around in his seat and Spirit rolled her eyes relentlessly. She looked over at Destiny, who was stunned to hear the tone in his voice, and motioned the words, "I'm sorry," with her lips. Destiny was appreciative of Spirit's attempt to rescue her from the nightmare that had so vividly become her reality. Destiny was overwhelmed by Epic's different personalities. It seemed as though she was meeting a new ego by the minute. The person that she fell in love with back in Houston had become a complete stranger.

8

THE SHADE

The car pulled up behind a tall brick office building. It was after hours, so the building was closed and the parking lot was dark.

"This will be our meeting spot" Epic said as he observed their surroundings. "Pay attention to your phones and listen for my texts. We'll be in the area, but just in case we lose sight, remember this spot."

Destiny took a deep breath. Her anxiety increased as she saw a pack of people crowded together in the parking lot adjacent to the tall brick building. They were gathered like seagulls on a beach. Every now and then one would stray into the dark allies that surrounded the buildings. Destiny could hear outbursts of profanity and wicked bolts of laughter. She rolled her window up and unlocked the car door.

The four girls got out of the car and split up into two groups of two – Destiny was with the young one. Spirit looked at Destiny and gave her two thumbs up as she took off with the older new face.

"We're going to check out the area. Don't worry, we'll be close," Epic stuttered, choking on the smoke fuming from his cigarette.

The brown car drove off. Destiny and the young new face stood in the dark of the abandoned parking lot. Destiny stood there like a bump on a log, stiff and motionless, and she could hear her heart thump like drums in her ear.

"This is not what I signed up for. What did I get myself into?" she muttered under her breath.

"Well let's go!" the young new face said anxiously tugging on Destiny's arm.

"Calm down!" Destiny snapped, snatching her arm away.

Destiny could hear the profanities in the adjacent parking lot get louder and closer. Three men clothed in darkness approached the two girls like shadows. Destiny didn't even notice when they separated from the pack of wolves that was bunched across the street.

"Well, well," one of the wolves said as he blew smoke into Destiny's face. It wasn't a cigarette. "You two look like you need a ride," he continued.

Destiny glanced out of the corner of her eyes to see if Spirit and her pupil were in sight, but all she could see was a glimpse of night fall. Spirit and her pupil were nowhere to be seen, nor were Epic and Zee

"What are two young beauties like yourselves doing out here in the dark?" another wolf asked. "It is way too dangerous out here. You girls need to get home."

The wolf sounded concerned, but Destiny knew better. Destiny remained calm and forced her eyes to focus on something else. She looked at the tall office buildings, then the sky, and then the trees. She knew that she could not let her eyes meet with the wolves – that was one thing that both Spirit and Epic warned her about, and she heard their voices in her head loud and clear.

The young new face focused her attention on her feet. She apparently knew better than to make eye contact as well. It was one of the biggest rules on *that* kind of street, and all the ladies who worked that kind of street were familiar with the rule. It was rule number one in the greed manual: "Never look another man in the eyes, other than your own." Every girl working *that* kind of street had that quote instilled in her memory. They also knew that the word "man" replaced the horrific truth of the word "pimp," which is exactly what Epic had become to Destiny, whether she believed it or not.

The three wolves moved in a little closer. Destiny's pupils were glued to a figment of her imagination that bounced off the walls of the tall office buildings. Destiny followed the figment carefully as she blocked the voices of the wolves. The last thing she needed was to be abducted by the wolves and be forced into joining their pack. She would not break. Destiny refused to make eye contact and resisted every attempt by the wolves to try and get her to do so.

When they realized she would not be moved, they targeted their attention to the young knew face who was still staring nervously at her feet. Her knees buckled together as she felt the three sets of eyes scoping her body. Destiny managed to ease her hand into her purse, without them noticing, and fumbled around for her mace spray. She clenched the can in her fingers as the wolves began to interrogate the young new face.

"You don't have to be scared lil' bit," the wolf with the concerned voice said gently to the young new face, "we're just trying to help you."

"Let's go, we're losing money," another said, annoyed that neither girl would budge.

Two of the wolves turned to walk away, leaving the one with the concerned voice behind.

"Alright lil' bit," he called the young new face, "I'll leave you alone." He took a step back and turned to join the other wolves, flicking his cigarette on the ground.

He stopped and turned back around to face the young new face, "All games aside, and just for the record, you really are beautiful." He turned again to walk away.

"Thank you," the young new face mumbled under her breath.

The wolf stopped in his tracks and rushed back to the young new face. "WHAT?" he screamed as spit sprayed out of his mouth all over her face.

Destiny, who still had her hand clenched around the small can of mace, was frozen. Her other hand managed to grab the arm of the young new face and the two girls backed up one step after the other as the wolf, now joined by the other two wolves, charged at them screaming profanities.

"WHAT DID YOU SAY?" they yelled. "THANK YOU? I'LL SHOW YOU THANK YOU," they threatened with their voices raised to the top of their lungs.

The young new face tried desperately to put her head back down, but it was too late. She had already broken rule number two: Never speak to another man. Destiny tightened her grip around the young new face's arm as they prepared to run. The wolves yelled louder and louder, and Destiny could see the saliva dripping from their mouths; still, she refused to look them in their eyes. I took my place and positioned myself directly in front of Destiny and stared the wolves straight in their eyes. The voices lowered.

"Man, let's go," one of the wolves said. "They're not worth much anyway."

The three wolves threw a few more profane insults to the girls and then turned and walked away. Destiny was deafened by the rapid beat of her heart that pierced her eardrums.

"Let's go," Destiny said, still holding the young new face's arm.

The two ran off into the night without direction – all they knew was that they had to get out of there.

9
THE BLACKOUT

Before they knew it, Destiny and the young new face had made it in front of a small dingy motel. Cars pulled in and out of the parking lot and the drivers ran in and out of the rooms with their heads down, as though they were hiding their faces from paparazzi cameras. A couple of girls paced the alley beside the motel back and forth. One played with the curls in her hair and the other anxiously chewed on a plastic straw. Destiny and the young new face found a secluded corner beside the motel where they could face the alley and see their surroundings.

"I'm sorry about what happened back there," the young new face apologized.

"No big deal," Destiny shrugged her shoulders. "Just don't talk to anyone else. Let's just get this over with quietly."

The young new face nodded her head. "I've been doing this for two years now you know."

Destiny made a fist and covered her nose, trying to shield the strong smell of urine coming from the corner where they stood. She ignored the young new face's attempt at a conversation. Destiny had a one track mind which led to the fastest way home. She couldn't care less to hear another sob story. Destiny's only focus was getting through this nightmare and getting home.

"I started when I was thirteen. My dad got me into it," the girl continued. "I left his sorry butt back in Arizona, though."

Destiny sighed.

The young new face kept talking. "I flew down here with a keeper, but one day I went back to his house and it was empty – up and went to Vegas without me, with some new broad."

"So you're by yourself down here?" Destiny asked. She could feel her heart breaking all over again as she realized she was having a conversation with a fifteen year old child.

"I sure am," the girl responded. "Nothing new though – I've been by myself all my life. The old man was just shelter and a way to eat after my mom died, know what I mean?"

Destiny nodded. "I hear you … but he's not looking for you?" she asked.

"Nah, I'm the last thing on his mind. I can tell you're a rookie though" the young new face said as she smiled and winked at a car passing by.

"Me?" Destiny asked with an attitude. "You're the one that almost got us killed back there. I may be a rookie, but I got a whole lot more sense than what you're working with."

Just then, a strange car pulled up in front of the two girls.

"That was my mistake," the young new face said as she walked towards the car. "You'll make a couple of those in these streets. Trust me, two years is like a lifetime in this game. I know what I'm doing. You be careful out here. Good luck!"

The young new face got into the strange car and disappeared as the car turned the corner of the motel. Destiny knew that the two were not supposed to split up, but she didn't want to make a fuss in front of the strange car. Besides, the young new face gave her no time to argue. Deep down she knew she would never see the face of the young girl again.

Destiny stood there in the urine drenched corner nervously gnawing at her acrylic finger nails. Another strange car pulled up in front of her. Destiny took a deep breath and approached the vehicle with a plastic smile. I looked up wanting so badly to stop her, but I had to let her go.

She went numb and got into to the strange car. It drove to the other side of the motel and parked behind an old green dumpster. Destiny watched as stray cats jumped out of it with pieces of trash in their mouths. That would be her focal point as she subconsciously removed herself from her body – all that would be left was flesh. Flesh that had become evil's playground.

Destiny fixated her mind on the stray cats climbing out of the dirty green trash can stonewalling the malicious ambush that devoured the innermost personal parts of her flesh. She separated mind from body as the poison of fornication invaded her soul. Destiny hadn't even noticed when the stranger had finished gallivanting around her corrupted body. The blackout quickly ended as Destiny found herself huddled in a corner. The brick wall scraped her back as vapors of urine caressed her nostrils. This time, she didn't cover her nose. The urine did not bother her anymore. To Destiny, she belonged in that corner. The trash piled up against the building of the old motel, was to Destiny, a mirror image of her existence.

I looked up again, praying that I could rescue her from the worthless thoughts that corrupted her mind, but I knew my position was to obey He whom had sent me; if He allowed it, there was purpose. I had to let her go. Another car pulled up beside Destiny, and again, she went numb. The cycle continued over and over again for the duration of the night. Destiny subconsciously watched herself from outside of her body in disgust as she repeated the thoughtless acts that had begun to define who she was. Disgust turned into anger, and anger into hatred. Destiny could no longer even stand the thought of who she had become. To her, it was there on those urine, garbage-filled streets that she belonged. The thoughts had won Destiny was lost.

She walked aimlessly down the dark streets of downtown Dallas. She was exhausted physically, but more so mentally, and was emotionally dry. She had lost her cell phone trying to defend herself during one of her many encounters that night and had no idea what time it was. It was either really late at night or really early in the morning, because fewer cars passed her by now. She had not seen the young new face for hours and was convinced she had run away. The only faces she had seen all night were the faces of strangers attacking her body. After a while, all the strangers started to look alike and each possessed the same personality and motive.

Destiny stopped in front of a convenient store and leaned against the rusty metal fence that surrounded it. She bent down to fix a strap on her shoe that had come loose from walking so much.

"You lost ma'?" a voice came from behind Destiny.

Destiny raised her head to see a tall skinny female in six-inch stilettos standing behind her.

"I'm good." Destiny continued fixing the strap on her shoe.

Rule number three: Never get too friendly with the competition, aka other working girls. They always have a motive.

The tall skinny woman had a motive, indeed, as she continued, "Who are you out here with?"

Destiny stood up and put her hand on her hip, looking passed the tall skinny female who was now standing in front of her. Destiny responded by stating The Charming's street name and brushed the female off as if the woman was beneath her.

"Well," The tall skinny female continued, "if you ever want better, give us a call." She held out a business card with the name of her 'employer' on it and tried to give it to Destiny.

"I'm good," Destiny stated as she walked away, leaving the female holding the card in her hand.

Just then a car pulled up in front of Destiny, full speed. The brakes screeched as it came to a halting stop. It was the brown car. Zee looked at Destiny with a worried look on his face as he flicked his cigarette out of the window. Epic was in his assigned seat on the passenger side, and in the back were Spirit and the older new face. Spirit had her head in her lap like she was sleeping. The older new face glanced at Destiny and then nervously looked away. Destiny was too exhausted to notice the anger on Epic's face, and frankly, she did not care. She opened the car door and plopped down in the back seat immediately removing her shoes. It was silent for about ten minutes as Zee maneuvered through the streets of downtown Dallas. It was not until they approached the freeway that Epic decided to break the silence.

"So where were you?" he asked, awkwardly calm.

"Working," Destiny replied.

"Where's the girl?" he asked.

"She took off."

"How much?" he said extending his hand to the back seat where Destiny was.

Sprit put her head up and watched as Destiny grabbed a wad of money from the tiny black purse still strapped across her chest.

"Not sure," Destiny responded, handing him the money. She swung her head back on the head rest and closed her eyes.

Spirit waited curiously as Epic counted the money in the front seat. She anxiously awaited his response as he shuffled through the bills. His cheek bones rose as a grin laced his face. Spirit smiled as though she was relieved and put her head back down in her lap.

"Good job baby girl," he said smiling at the money in his hands.

Destiny did not respond. Her mind was far, far away in a totally different place – a place far away from the world she was actually in.

The bright yellow lights from the hotel sign awoke all three girls who had fallen asleep in the back seat of the brown car. They squinted as they rubbed their eyes, annoyed at being disturbed from their twenty-minute nap. Even Zee looked tired, but Epic was still glowing with contentment.

"Awesome night ladies," he said as the car pulled into its designated space. "Come on, let's go over everything."

The sun had begun to peak through the clouds. Destiny was in disbelief that she had been awake for an entire night, with the exception of her car ride nap. All three girls, including the older new face, grunted at the fact that Epic actually wanted to have a discussion at this hour.

"Just real quick," he added.

The three exhausted girls went into the downstairs suite and each found a spot comfortably on the couch. Zee sat on the recliner, and Epic stood in front of the television facing the group like he was about to give a speech. He talked about how much money the girls made and reiterated how good of a job they did. He discussed their goals and promised that they would return home at the end of the two weeks. He spoke about their goals when they returned for the three months as well, but Destiny tuned that part out as she knew she would not be coming back.

He told them that he had tried to call the new young face on her cell phone, but it was obvious that she decided to join another crew since she wasn't answering his calls. That frustrated him, and he called Destiny forward to question her about what happened. Destiny assured him that she had no knowledge that the girl would run off and informed him of her cocky attitude towards knowing the 'game' so well, as she put it.

"Okay, so you didn't think to call me when she took off like that?" Epic interrupted as Destiny pled her case.

"For what? It was work. I figured she'd come right back. It's not like she's not familiar with all this," Destiny said raising her voice.

She had become frustrated by Epic's questions and responded to him like he was the same guy that she met in Houston. She was quickly reminded that he was not.

Destiny could feel her face go numb as the back of his hand stung her face. She was in shock as she stood motionless trying to collect herself. Spirit put her hand over her mouth and turned to look at the wall. The older new face didn't flinch – she appeared to be used to this kind of abuse. Zee covered his disbelief by lighting another cigarette. Destiny looked Epic directly in his eyes as a tear trickled down her swollen face. It was evident that he could not stand the hurt that ejected from her eyes as he looked away.

"Go in the room," he said with the bass still in his voice.

Destiny turned and went into the small back room and sat on the bed. Tears streamed down her face at the thought that this beast was once a man that she had fallen so deeply in love with; a man that had manipulated her heart and victimized her kindness. Yet, the only person that she could think to blame was herself.

"How could I let this happen?" she whispered.

Destiny could hear the front door of the suite open and close and heard footsteps trample up the stairs to the room above her. Zee and the older new face had left. She stared through the window of the hotel suite as the tears continued to flood her eyes. She did not bother to look when she heard the room door shut, she did not bother to look when Spirit flopped down on the bed beside her – she just continued to stare blankly out of the window trying to distance herself from what had just happened.

"You ok Hun?" Spirit asked softly as she handed Destiny a sheet of tissue.

Destiny nodded.

"I've gotten plenty of those," Spirit said jokingly.

"I just can't believe he would do something like that. I mean, him? To me?"

"I know it sucks. But one more week and you can kiss his sorry tail good riddance," Sprit said, dabbing an ice pack on Destiny's face. "Well, don't kiss his tail. Just kick it," Spirit teased.

Destiny smiled and nodded her head as she wiped the tears from her cheeks. There was a light tap on the room door before it swung open. Destiny was nauseous as she looked at Epic standing in the doorway of the room.

"Hey let me talk to her for a second," he said to Spirit.

Spirit handed Destiny the ice pack and reluctantly left the room. Destiny quickly dried her tears and looked into Epic's eyes as he began to ramble.

"I had to do that," he said, "I had to let the new girl know that I mean business."

"So you slap me in the face to do it?"

Epic knelt down in front of Destiny and folded his hands together in her lap. He called her by her real name, not Destiny.

"Please understand, I'm just playing the part. I had to. This whole thing is getting to me I guess. Seeing you out there... I just want to reach our goal and get out before we get sucked in."

Destiny had no words for him. It had been a while since he had addressed her by her birth name so he did have her attention, but no words. She listened quietly as he apologized repeatedly. She could see a shadow in the crack by the room door – she knew it was Spirit eaves dropping on their conversation. Destiny struggled to find words for Epic, who was still slumped in her lap asking for forgiveness.

"What about Spirit?" she mumbled.

"What about her?"

"I think you should pull her out. I know a little bit about her past and I don't think she wants to do this anymore," Destiny said, trying to reason with Epic.

"She'll be okay – she's a vet. This is her lifestyle, and she knows way more than you and I both."

"But I think she's tired. I don't think she can last mentally *or* emotionally. I think she's..."

"She must have gotten to you," he interrupted. "Look, Spirit is not like you. She's tough. She can handle all of this. It's you that I'm concerned about. This is not for you, I see that now. Trust me, she'll last another week, another year if you let her," he laughed.

Destiny looked over at the crack in the door. The shadow stood still for a few seconds and then disappeared.

10

THE INVASION

Destiny had managed to completely stray away from her feelings as the world she had become a part of consumed her conscience and emotions. Every emotion had to be demolished in order for Destiny to endure the hell that she now found herself in. She was fully detached from reality as she spent the rest of the week mocking a fantasy in the presence of different strangers. Epic did not make her go back on the dark streets of downtown, but he did not hesitate to invite strangers to the once cozy hotel suite either. Destiny remained in her dark zone and eventually everything became a blur to her. She could no longer distinguish night from day, let alone what day of the week it was. She had no idea that it was already Thursday and that she was one day closer to going home, so when Epic brought it to her attention, she was elated.

"I'm thinking we can leave bright and early Saturday morning. The room is paid for until noon," he said as he crunched on a bowl of cereal.

"Sounds good," Destiny responded as she glared into the sixty-inch television. She did not want Epic to know how excited she was out fear that he would figure out her plan and change his mind. Destiny pretended to be so comfortable with her new lifestyle when Epic was around. She had him fooled enough to believe that she would return for an additional three months as she promised in the beginning, but Destiny had other plans. She could not wait to return home and take off the garments of filth that she had covered herself with for the past two weeks.

"The baby's coming."

"What?" Destiny broke her focus and looked at Epic.

He finished chewing the cereal in his mouth and continued, "She'll be here today. The babysitter had an emergency, so she's coming down here."

Destiny couldn't believe it. How could someone bring a newborn baby in such an environment?

"Is Spirit okay with that?" she asked.

"She will be. It's my baby too, so she really doesn't have a say. Having the baby here will cheer her up a little bit, anyway."

"Wow," Destiny replied rubbing her forehead with one hand and her leg with the other.

"So, he went to go get her?" Destiny asked, referring to Zee.

"Yeah, he left this morning. He should be here soon."

Destiny continued rubbing her head and her thigh – it was a nervous habit that she had picked up as a child, and she was definitely nervous. She did not know why, but the thought of an innocent child being in the midst of all of this corruption worried her. Destiny felt a sharp pain dash through her head. She could hear footsteps coming down the stairs from the room above her. She heard Spirit's famous fake flirtatious giggle and then a car door shut. The car started and drove away.

"When is my baby getting here?" Spirit yelled bursting through the door. She handed Epic a small stack of money folded together.

"Should be here in about thirty minutes," he answered, taking the stash out of her hand.

Spirit threw herself onto the floor like a three year old having a temper tantrum. "I want my baby!" she screamed.

"On that note," Epic stood up, put the money in his pocket, and went into the main bedroom, slamming the door behind him.

For the past few days Destiny had noticed the tension that had built between Epic and Spirit. Spirit could hardly stand the sight of him and only spoke to him when she had a client. For days Destiny had played the mediator between the two. Both Epic and Spirit drew closer to Destiny as the two had begun to hate each other. Destiny was not sure when all the tension initially started, but she could feel it spiraling out of control. Spirit had become so unstable that all she did was cry and holler like a toddler; all Epic did was ignore it. Destiny, however, could not ignore it. She could tell that Spirit was breaking down, and quickly.

Destiny went over to Spirit who was still pounding her fists on the floor and placed her hand on her back. "Hey," Destiny said calmly.

Spirit raised her head off of the floor and smiled at Destiny, without a tear dripping from either of her eyes. It was as though she was a totally different person. Spirit looked over to the closed door that Epic had entered and began laughing.

"What in the world?" Destiny asked confused.

"Girl," Spirit said standing up as she brushed herself off, "that's just my way of getting rid of him."

"Really?" Destiny asked sarcastically.

Spirit took off to the back room and waved her hand for Destiny to follow. She closed the door behind Destiny and started whispering. "I can't even stand the sight of him," she said. Destiny looked into Spirit's eyes as she continued to vent. "All I see when I look at him now is just another evil man trying to get me. They all try to get me. I think he's trying to kill me."

"Spirit," Destiny said, trying to interrupt

"No, really. He knows about my past, yet he continues to sell me to these men. It will kill me if I have to watch another creepy hand slither up my thigh. It will kill me if I have to let another pair of crusty lips scratch my chest. It will kill me!"

Spirit had begun to hyperventilate; she struggled to catch her breath as she burst into tears. Destiny grabbed her into a hug and directed her to sit down on the bed. Tears flowed down Destiny's cheeks as her heart immersed with the pain she felt for Spirit. This was no longer a game. I stood back and watched keenly as Spirit poured out her soul.

"I'm tired Destiny, just so tired. I've been fighting men ever since I learned to walk; evil, greedy men. I don't even know what a good man looks like," Spirit choked, trying to get her words out.

"Spirit, you can't do this to yourself," Destiny said, rubbing Spirit's back. "You are beautiful and have a whole lifetime to find happiness. Let go of your past and grab on to your future – there is so much out there for you."

Spirit sobbed as she listened to Destiny's wisdom.

Destiny continued, "This stops now. He can slap us around if he wants to, but we both know that he can't force us to do anything. He can't force you to do this any longer."

"He's not going to want to hear that," Sprit sobbed.

"Well he's going to have to. I'll talk to him."

"Yeah, he loves you anyway. He hates me."

"Love?" Destiny yelled. "You call this love? Sweetie, this is far from love. He doesn't know the meaning of the word."

"I heard him apologize to you the other day, for slapping you. He's never done that with anyone. Not even me."

Destiny laughed, "Well if that's what you call love, then we have a lot to learn when we leave this place."

Spirit cracked a smile and mumbled, "You're all I have, you know. You're like my best friend. You're my *only* friend."

Destiny held Spirit a little tighter, and together they cried.

Thirty minutes had gone by and Spirit managed to dose off into a deep sleep. Destiny placed a thin blanket over her sleeping friend and quietly snuck out of the room. She was extra careful not to wake her because she knew that Spirit had not slept for the past few days. Destiny knew that Spirit was only taking ten-minute catnaps throughout the days, and at this point, rest was critical.

Destiny went into the living room where Epic was back on the couch.

"Is psycho asleep?" he laughed

"Spirit is sleeping," Destiny replied in a serious tone.

"Well good, because I got her three appointments for tonight. Big money too," he gloated.

Destiny went over to the couch and sat right beside him. He placed his arm over her and pulled her head towards his chest. Destiny jerked her head and removed his arm from around her.

"What's your deal?" he asked, shocked by her reaction.

"We need to talk."

He removed the gold framed glasses from his face and rubbed his eyes. "About what?" he sighed.

"I don't think we should wait until Saturday to leave, I think we should leave now."

"Now? It's five o'clock in the evening. We'll be in rush hour traffic," he said with a grin.

"I'm serious!"

"Okay, okay. What happened?"

"It's just time to go. We surpassed our goal, and there's no reason for us to stay. Spirit really needs a break from all of this."

"Spirit? Oh Lord," he said, rolling his eyes.

"Seriously, she's not doing well at all. I think we should get her home ASAP. We can leave tomorrow morning."

Epic saw how serious Destiny was as he studied her face. He sighed, "I got some business to take care of in the morning. We can leave after that I guess."

Destiny smiled, "Thank you."

The doorknob rattled, followed by a light knock at the door. Zee entered carrying what appeared to be a pint sized porcelain package. In his hands was a tiny baby dressed in a frilly pink dress with a matching pacifier dangling from her mouth. Her lace headband was the identical shade of pink and perfectly enclosed the soft, shiny curls that covered her head. It was the most beautiful sight that Destiny had laid eyes on in a while.

"Well hello, Daddy's baby!" Epic said, taking the infant out of Zee's hands.

"Now that's the kind of kid I want. She was quiet the entire way," Zee said, looking for a spot to place the baby bags.

"She's just cool like her daddy," Epic said cooing at the baby.

"She is gorgeous," Destiny uttered.

"Again, like her daddy. Here hold her," Epic said passing Destiny the small child.

Destiny readily took the baby and cradled her. She fell in love with the child by the second as the baby looked up at Destiny with her big brown eyes. Holding the baby reminded Destiny of how much she missed her own children. She wanted nothing more than to be with them at that very moment. Spirit had awoken from her sleep and heard all of the commotion from the back room. She rushed into the living room to meet her baby. "Come here, mommy's pumpkin tot," she said snatching the infant out of Destiny's arms. She held the baby close to her chest and danced around the room, loudly singing a made-up lullaby out of tune.

"Calm down!" Epic snapped, "Stop acting crazy."

The baby started to cry, but Spirit just sang louder, ignoring Epic. Destiny and Zee looked at each other as the baby's scream got louder and louder.

"You're making her cry. Give her to me, what is wrong with you?" Epic asked, trying not to yell in front of the child.

"STOP TRYING TO TAKE HER AWAY FROM ME!" Spirit screamed from the top of her lungs. The baby, now startled, paused and then continued to scream, increasing her pitch. "YOU'RE TURNING HER AGAINST ME. YOU'RE TRYING TO TAKE EVERYTHING AWAY FROM ME!"

Spirit ran into the back room with the baby still in her arms and slammed the door. Epic took off after her, but Destiny stopped him.

"I'll go," Destiny said calmly.

"I don't know what her problem is, but get my baby away from that psycho."

Destiny went into the room and found the bed, where Spirit usually ran to, empty. The closet door was closed and she could hear the baby's cries from behind it. Destiny slowly opened the door to find Spirit huddled in the corner trying to console the crying infant with her pacifier. Destiny moved a set of clothes dangling from a hanger so that she could get a clear view of Spirit's face.

"Spirit," she said gently.

"What?" Spirit hollered.

"Let me help you," Destiny said extending her arms to take the baby.

Spirit did not resist as Destiny carefully slid the child out of Spirit's arms and into her own. The child almost immediately stopped crying.

"She likes you," Spirit whimpered. "I think she hates me."

"She doesn't hate you, you're her mother. She was probably crying because of all of the yelling."

"Well I'm not yelling now," Spirit said taking her child back from Destiny. The baby began to cry. Destiny was speechless as Spirit shoved the child back into her arms.

"See?" Spirit said spitefully.

"It's because you're all upset. Babies can feel that kind of stuff."

Spirit rested her forehead on her knees and began to sob profusely. Destiny put the baby over her shoulder and patted her softly on her back. "We're going home tomorrow," Destiny said with a reassuring smile.

Spirit lifted her head and cracked a grin. "Tomorrow?"

"Yep. We're out of here, and tomorrow will mark the beginning of your new life – no more of this garbage."

Spirit frowned, "But you're going to leave me. I know it, and then I'll be stuck with him all by myself."

"I'll be there for you, Spirit. I'll help you through this," Destiny promised.

Spirit smiled.

Destiny spent the rest of the night tending to the infant, who had already become attached to her. Destiny was the only person that the baby would be content with. She screamed with her mother, and she screamed with her father. It was like the child only felt safe in Destiny's arms. Spirit and Epic hadn't uttered a single word to each other; each pretended that the other did not exist. Spirit continued singing her off-tune songs while Epic spent the night counting and recounting his money. Zee was asleep on the recliner because he had already turned in the key to the room upstairs. The older young face hadn't been seen in days – it was obvious that she had run away too, as did every girl that started out on Epic's undermining mission.

Destiny placed the sleeping baby into her car seat and pulled it close to the bed. Spirit had made the closet her hideout and was asleep in her comfortable corner behind the clothes. Destiny slid under her blanket and stared at the ceiling. She looked at the closet where Spirit slept, looked at the car seat, and then back at the ceiling. Destiny could not shake the feeling that had come over her – it was a fearful feeling, like something bad was going to happen. She felt bad for Spirit, but did not know how to help her. There was a short squeal as the room door eased open. Epic inched in toward the car seat.

"I want her to sleep with me tonight," he said picking up the car seat.

Destiny nodded nervously as she stared at the closet door in hopes that Spirit would not wake up.

"We'll leave around noon," he whispered as he left the room with the baby.

Destiny rolled over and put the blanket over her face. "God," she prayed silently, "I know I'm the last person you want to hear from right now, but please God, I need you. Please protect that child, and if you have time, please protect me too."

Destiny closed her eyes and drifted off to sleep. Those were the words that I had been waiting on for so long. I looked up and smiled. Help was on the way – it was time.

It must have been about four o'clock in the morning when Destiny began to toss and turn. She could not seem to get comfortable. Out of nowhere her heart began to race; she broke out into a cold sweat and felt like she was drowning. Destiny threw the blanket from her face and sat up in the bed gasping for air. It was dark, but Destiny could see a silhouette directly in front of her. She reached for the lamp on the nightstand and flicked the switch. There stood Spirit, staring at her and smiling.

"You scared me," Destiny panted, grabbing her chest.

"I couldn't sleep," Spirit replied, crawling into the bed next to Destiny.

"What's wrong?" Destiny asked.

"Where's the baby?"

"She's with her dad. What's wrong?"

"It's back."

"What's back?" Destiny asked, still trying to catch her breath.

"The feeling," Spirit said, cuddling under the covers. She laid her head on Destiny's shoulder.

"What feeling?"

"Death."

Destiny could not find the words to respond, so she lay there quietly as Spirit fell asleep on her shoulder. Destiny left the night lamp on and stared blankly at the ceiling. "Dear God," she whispered. She knew something was about to happen, something big – she felt it in her bones. She felt it in her spirit. I motioned to the others. Our swords rose.

11

THE TAKEOVER

The sunlight came beaming through the blinds and bounced off of Destiny's face. She rubbed her eyes, jumped out of bed, and headed towards the yelling that was coming from the living room. When did she fall asleep? She planned to stay awake and keep an eye on Spirit after her bizarre comment last night. A part of her felt like she was in a dream as she darted confusedly out of the bedroom. The living area was a mess. There were items thrown everywhere, from food to shoes. It looked like the place had been ransacked.

"What is going on?" she asked loudly.

Spirit was in the process of throwing a stack of CD's at Epic who ducked swiftly out of the way.

"He's trying to kill me!" Spirit screamed.

"She's nuts!" Epic yelled back.

Destiny went over to Spirit and snatched the stack of compact discs out of her hands.

"He sold my baby!" Spirit proceeded to holler.

"She's nuts!" Epic repeated.

Destiny grabbed Spirit's hand, "Calm down. Where is the baby?" she asked Epic.

"She's on her way back to Houston! She's going to my mom's house, away from this looney tune!"

Destiny looked around. The baby's bags were gone, and so was Zee. Destiny glanced out of the door, which was open. The brown car was gone. Destiny knew Epic would never put his child in harm's way and was convinced by his story.

"Okay. Let's go put some clothes on and hit the road. You can meet your baby back home," Destiny said, trying to reassure a frantic Spirit.

"No, he stole her! I have to go get her!" Spirit screamed.

She tugged her hand away from Destiny and bolted outside. She ran into the parking lot, still screaming, and one of her feet went into a pothole. She tripped and her face smacked the concrete. Destiny and Epic ran outside and each grabbed an arm, assisting her to her feet. Destiny was in shock by Spirit's actions. Everything seemed to happen so fast.

"Let me go!" Spirit yelled, pulling away the arm held by Epic. He and Destiny exchanged eye contact in disbelief and confusion.

Destiny helped Spirit back inside and led her to the backroom. Spirit threw herself on the bed and slung the blanket over her face. Destiny watched as Spirit dozed off into a slumber, as though nothing had happened. Five minutes had not passed before there was a knock at the room door – it was Epic.

"Hey, um, the cops are here. Someone heard all that commotion."

Destiny rubbed her forehead and thighs.

He continued as he puffed on a cigarette, "I told them she's having a breakdown and needs help. They're going to take her."

"Take her wh…"

Before Destiny could finish her question, Spirit popped up from under the covers.

"No," She pleaded with her voice lowered, "don't let them take me. Please don't let him do this."

"Can't we just take her home? We can take her somewhere out there."

Smoke gathered around Epic's face and he coughed. It was obvious that his nerves were getting the best of him. "She is crazy. She needs to go to the crazy house."

Destiny grabbed Epic by his hand and escorted him into the hallway. She whispered so that neither Spirit nor the cops waiting at the door would hear her. "Please. We can't just put her in some psych ward way out here in Dallas. I agree she needs help, but she needs to be close to home. Let's just get to Houston."

Epic agreed and convinced the cops at the door that everything was all right. As was routine, they had to speak with Spirit before they left to make sure that the situation was under control. They entered the bedroom where she faked like she was asleep and questioned her.

"I was just upset. Sorry," Spirit said with her thumb in her mouth like a child.

The cops had no reason to investigate any further, so they left. As soon as they walked out of the door, Spirit let out a conniving sound of laughter. "Thank you," she said to Destiny in a snake-like voice. She immediately plopped back on to the bed and flung the sheets over her face.

Destiny stood still as she observed Spirit's deceiving actions. She felt something deep in her gut. She heard her grandmother's voice in her head – her discernment had kicked in. She was speechless, but the only word her tongue would allow her to utter was "Jesus." My strength immediately increased. I felt the power, and the others did too.

"Jesus," she said out loud as she ran into the living room where Epic was gathering his bags. "We have to leave," she said frantically.

"I know. Get your stuff together and let's bounce."

"You don't understand. We have to leave now."

Destiny stopped in her speech. She was distracted by a huge cockroach that crept from under the couch. She looked at the ceiling and saw another. She looked over to the kitchen and saw another crawling on the refrigerator. Her heart began to pound – she had not spotted a single bug since they had been there, until now.

"Hello," Epic said snapping his fingers to regain her attention.

"We have to leave right now. We don't have time for stuff."

"Don't tell me you've gone crazy too," he smirked.

"Look, I know I haven't been your typical church girl lately, but I grew up in the church. I grew up with a praying grandmother and I know when something just isn't right."

Epic scratched his head in confusion. "What does church have to do with anything?"

"She's not just having a nervous breakdown in there. It's something way bigger than that."

"What?" Epic asked.

"I know you're not going to believe me, but just trust me enough to get out of here right now. That's no nervous breakdown, that girl is full of demons."

Epic laughed, "What so now you're saying she's possessed? Maybe you should have gone with those cops to the loony bin."

"Wow." He continued laughing.

Just then Spirit entered the room. I took my position and the others joined me. She went into the kitchen, grabbed a bottle of water from the refrigerator, and took three big gulps. Destiny and Epic observed closely.

"It's hot in here," she said.

Destiny and Epic looked over at the AC vent as cold air forced its way through.

"I've been thinking," Spirit continued, "we shouldn't leave yet. We're making too much money here and I'm just now starting to get comfortable." Another cockroach crept slowly on the ceiling above Spirit's head. This time Epic saw it too.

"It's time to go. You've done enough," he said.

"But we're just starting to have fun guys," Spirit grinned as she made her way over to the couch. She laid face down and again drifted off into a deep sleep.

Destiny felt her gut turning inside of her. She took a deep breath and repeatedly called on the name of Jesus inside her head. The only thing that she could think of was Ephesians 6:12 in the Bible, *"For we are not fighting against flesh and blood enemies, but against evil rulers and authorities of the unseen world, against mighty powers in this dark world, and against evil spirits in the heavenly places"* - and she knew exactly what meant. It was time.

Destiny rushed over to the coffee table and picked up the burgundy Bible that sat on top. Epic followed her lead and stood right next to her. He, too, was forced to go back to his roots. His grandfather was a pastor, and every lady in his family was a prayer warrior. He also felt the tugging in his gut.

Destiny briskly flipped through the pages of the Bible. She turned to Psalms 23, Psalms 91, and Isaiah 54 and read all the scriptures out loud as Epic repeated every word after her. Destiny was in a panic. She wasn't sure if God would come to her rescue after she had betrayed Him so disgustingly, but she knew He at least heard her. She heard her grandmother's voice in her head that repeatedly said: "Keep praying." Destiny continued to call on the name of Jesus, but she now found herself professing it with her tongue instead of just in her head. Epic continued to follow her lead as he too called the name Jesus.

"What are y'all doing?" Spirit asked, laughing hysterically.

She got up from the couch and moved toward Destiny and Epic, whose backs were against the door. As she approached them, she spoke in what sounded like three different languages at one time.

"Well, well, well, what do we have here? Preacher pimp and minister prostitute," Spirit laughed harder.

Destiny knew that it was not Spirit laughing, and it was not her talking – it was not Spirit, it was a demonic spirit. Destiny confidently stared into the black, cold, eyes imbedded in Spirit's once beautiful face. "Let's go now. You can't fool me and I will not be fooled by you," Destiny said boldly.

Epic stood back and listened nervously. He did not understand what was going on, but he believed Destiny's version of the story. Spirit laughed even harder, this time in a different, much deeper tone, as her zombie-like body paced closer and closer to Destiny. Destiny did not move and did not break eye contact. Spirit planted herself right in front of Destiny and let out an unimaginable high-pitched screech – the kind that is usually only heard in movies. Destiny felt like she had been hit in the stomach by a baseball soaring full speed. Her lungs felt like they had collapsed, and the back of her throat tightened. Her ears rung as she waited for the deafening sound to end. Destiny felt the spirit of fear overtake her as chill bumps covered her petite body. I yelled as loud as I could for her to get out.

"We have to go!" Destiny yelled, frenziedly running out of the front door.

She ran to the little silver car and rested her hand on the trunk, wheezing for air. Epic scurried to her side.

"What the heck was that?" he asked.

"Evil," she panted.

"Wow," he replied in a state of shock. "I felt it."

Destiny leaned against the car for a couple of minutes trying to catch her breath.

"Jesus," I whispered in her ear.

"Jesus," she repeated.

"Go," I said softly. I knew that destruction was near – Destiny had to leave Dallas, and quickly.

"We have to go now," Destiny said bouncing off car.

"How are we going to leave with her acting like that?" Epic asked.

Destiny paused as she looked at the window of the room where Spirit stood, boring her eyes from behind the curtain. All that Destiny could see were those eyes. They had to leave.

"By faith," Destiny answered. She turned to Epic and grabbed both of his hands. "We're going to have to stick together and you're going to have to trust me," she said firmly.

He nodded and together they stood in the parking lot of the hotel and prayed. More help came. Destiny felt a sudden boost of confidence. A super natural peace cloaked her entire body inside and out. Hand in hand, Destiny and Epic walked back towards the room. There, Spirit marked her place by the window and watched as they eventually approached her.

"We have to go now Spirit," Destiny said in a calm reassuring voice.

Spirit stubbornly refused to move and rolled her eyes. Destiny put her hand out and tried again.

"Let's go," she said warmly.

Spirit crossed her arms and stomped out of the room. Destiny and Epic managed to get Spirit into the back seat of the small silver coupe. Destiny felt uneasy with having Spirit sit behind her, so she climbed into the back instead of on the passenger side.

"What about our stuff?" Epic asked as he started the engine.

"We have no time for that," Destiny responded, "let's go home."

12

THE BATTLE

The car pulled out of the hotel parking lot and merged onto the freeway. My help and I followed closely behind. Our strength increased by the number. There were dozens of us now covering and protecting my assignment. There were also dozens of them, from darkness, trying to bring her down. We were ready.

They had not even made it out of Dallas yet before Spirit started acting up. Signs of a nervous breakdown eventually began to manifest as Spirit's personalities changed by the minute. Destiny kept her cool as she sat right next to Spirit, listening to the many voices stream out of her mouth. One minute Spirit imitated the voice of a four year old child, who only wanted to lay on Destiny with her thumb in her mouth. The next minute she was an angry prostitute with raging hormones that only wanted to talk about intercourse. There was even a moment where Spirit took the role of a man and had become masculine as she slouched in the back seat complaining about how hot it was. Destiny was not shaken. She blocked out the attempts of Spirit and her spirits to intimidate her – that was until Destiny heard the most horrifying voices of them all.

Epic was smoking a cigarette to add to the pile of cigarette butts in his ashtray that had accumulated within the past hour. The 4-year-old personality asked him to stop smoking. He ignored it. The masculine personality politely asked Epic not to smoke around the 4-year-old. He ignored it. Then came the voice – the voice that nearly cracked the windows and rocked the car, causing Epic to lose control of the wheel. The cigarette fell out of his hand and into his lap. He quickly exited the freeway and swerved into an empty parking lot. Destiny was the first one out of the car as she bolted to the other side of the parking lot. Epic ran to catch her and clamped onto her arm.

"Did you hear that?" he hollered in disbelief.

Destiny shook her head vigorously. "I can't do this!" she screamed.

The two looked over at the car. Spirit was still inside, banging her fists against the window. She was yelling profanities and all of her personalities seemed to be screaming at the same time.

"I can't do this," Destiny repeated.

"We have to. We can't stay here," Epic said, staring at the out of control Spirit.

"But I can't," Destiny cried, "I'm not strong enough for this. This type of thing only happens in movies, not in real life. Not to me."

Epic wiped the tears falling from her eyes and gently said, "You're the strongest person I know. I don't understand what's going on but I do know that I can't make it through this without you. We have to stay strong."

Destiny was too hysterical to process what Epic was saying. Her bones were weak, and her mind was exhausted. She could not feel an ounce of strength in her body. The banging from the car got louder as Spirit was now using her feet to hit the glass windows. Epic rushed to the car to try and calm her.

Destiny could not move; she could not bring herself to get back into that car. Instead, she reached for the cell phone tucked into her back pocket. She felt ashamed and like an outcast. She was convinced that no one she called would want to speak to her, or would even believe her. But she had to call someone; she felt like she could not do this alone. But I was near. Though she could not see me, I and the other angels were near.

Destiny frantically started dialing numbers in her phone. She needed to reach someone that had enough faith to understand and believe what she was going through.

"Good afternoon. How can I help you," the voice on the other line said cheerfully. It was a prayer counselor from Destiny's church, Faith Tabernacle.

"I need help!" Destiny cried desperately.

Before giving the gentleman a chance to respond, Destiny went into a fearful rampage about her encounter with Spirit and her many personalities. She expressed to the prayer counselor how she knew that she was wrestling against things that her eyes could not see.

"Did you hear me?" she asked after she finished her outburst.

"Yes I did," the counselor replied, "and it just seems like maybe your friend is having some sort of breakdown that has you all nerved up. What I want you to do is just take a deep breath, and we can pray."

Destiny was unresponsive as she listened to the gentleman's impersonal prayer. It was evident that he did not believe her.

"There," he said when he was done. "How do you feel now?"

Destiny sighed and hung up the phone. There had to be someone that would help her. She scrolled down the list of numbers in her contacts and stopped at her mother's number. Just then she heard a honk. Epic was in the driver's seat waving for her to come on. Somehow, he had gotten Spirit to calm down.

Destiny looked passed Epic, into the back seat of the car. Her eyes met with evil as Spirit grinned wickedly. Destiny felt another bolt of fear rush her soul. She pressed the dial button on her cell phone as fast as she could.

"Hello," the voice answered.

Destiny immediately started screaming into the phone.

"Help me!" she screamed. "I can't do it! I need help"

"Calm down baby," the voice responded. It was her friend's mother, Mrs. Sue.

"I can't. It's going to kill us!"

Mrs. Sue got louder, "Calm down. What happened?"

Destiny told the story again, this time with more detail. She told about the personalities and the cold, black eyes that taunted her.

"Baby," Mrs. Sue said calmly, "you stop it right now." she continued, "The one thing it wants you to do is be afraid, so stop. You look that thing in the eyes and plea the blood of Jesus right now!"

Mrs. Sue began to pray for Destiny, who slowly regained her composure.

"Say it baby, say it. Say I plead the Blood of Jesus!" she said firmly.

"I plead the Blood of Jesus!" Destiny repeated.

"Say it again, I plead the Blood of Jesus!"

"I PLEAD THE BLOOD OF JESUS!" Destiny affirmed.

Destiny could feel the cloak of peace fall on her all over again. She felt a warm sensation, as though the blood of Jesus physically poured onto her body. I smiled. Destiny hung up the phone with the voice who was still praying on the other end. She walked boldly towards the car, but this time, she sat in the front seat. She was no longer afraid.

"Let's go," she told Epic, sliding her sunglasses over her eyes.

Spirit was slumped in the back seat, paralyzed as her muscles struggled to flinch. The disgusted look on her face implied that she wanted to put her hands around Destiny's neck as tight as she could, but she couldn't. She could not touch Destiny now, and this angered her. I smiled as the car headed back to Houston, but I knew that this journey was far from over.

13

THE ACT

Epic managed to make it into a little town outside of Dallas. It seemed like they had been driving for hours, but they had only made it to the outskirts of Dallas. Destiny stretched her feet and pointed her toes to try and relieve the cramping in her legs. The entire time she repeated quietly to herself what Mrs. Sue had encouraged her to say.

Destiny looked down at the cell phone still clenched in her hand. She was astonished to see the last call that was made. Destiny was certain that she had selected her mother's number, but the powerful voice that answered her desperate cry for help was definitely not her mother. Destiny smiled as she continued to stare at the phone number. How ironic that it happened to be Vision's mother that answered her call – the very friend that Destiny had betrayed. The same friend that she had not spoken to in months. The friend that tried to warn Destiny through actions of separation that trouble was on the way. "How ironic," Destiny thought.

"I have to potty," said the 4-year-old personality in the back seat.

"We can't stop. You'll use it when we get home," Epic responded.

"But I have to use it NOW!" Spirit demanded.

Epic did not pay attention to her and continued driving. Destiny observed. Spirit sat up at a ninety degree angle with her back perfectly straight. She looked at Epic and then at Destiny. All of a sudden she let out a loud, horrific screeching noise. It was the same screech that jolted Destiny once before. Spirit threw her back on the seat and began kicking and screaming. She violently tugged at her hair, snatching patches out at a time, and then began taking her clothes off as urine slowly filled the seat.

"Pull in over there!" Destiny yelled, pointing to a small church facing the freeway. The sign mounted on the lawn of the church read Mount Zion House of Praise.

Epic switched lanes, making his way over to the exit and quickly turned into the church parking lot of Mount Zion. Spirit was still in the back seat kicking and screaming. He pulled up right in front of the building. There were two older ladies dressed in white, standing at the entrance. Destiny hopped out of the car, startling the two women.

"We need help," Destiny said pointing to the car.

"Is someone hurt?" one of the women asked.

"Not yet," Destiny said in a panic.

Epic got out of the car and joined Destiny, who was trying to explain to the ladies what was going on.

"I think we need prayer," he said. "We need it bad."

The women escorted Destiny inside of the building into a small room right beside the sanctuary.

"I'll get Pastor Thompson," one of them said, handing Destiny a bottle of water.

Another lady handed her a towel to wipe her face, and gently rubbed her back. "Calm down. You came to the right place," the lady reassured.

Destiny could hear Spirit complaining on the other side of the door. Somehow the women, with the help of some ushers, managed to get the psychotic Spirit out of the car.

"There's nothing wrong with me," Destiny heard Spirit say.

Destiny took a deep sigh of exhaustion and put her head into her lap as the lady continued to rub her back. In a way, Destiny was relieved that they had found the little church, and was happy that she no longer had to do this alone. Finally someone would help her.

Destiny sat in the peaceful room for about thirty minutes with her head rested on her lap. The entire time the lady continued to rub Destiny's back. They were so kind to her and it was reassuring to know that they believed her.

"Well hello there."

Destiny picked her head up. The pastor of the church was pulling up a little folding chair in front of her.

"Hi," Destiny replied.

"I'm Pastor Thompson. So they tell me you've had a really rough day."

Destiny looked up at the old wooden clock hanging in the corner of the room. It was already eight o'clock at night. Destiny felt like she was in a twilight zone.

"Yes it has," she responded sitting up in the chair.

"Your friend happens to be my nephew."

Destiny was confused.

"Yes, yes," the pastor continued, "just so happens that his grandfather is my uncle. Small world, right?"

"Indeed," Destiny responded.

"Now your other friend…"

"She's not my friend," Destiny interrupted. "I don't know who or what that is!"

The pastor smiled. "It's a miracle you guys made it this far. She was in need of serious help."

"Was?" Destiny asked.

"My prayer team and I have been praying for her since you guys got here. There was a breakthrough. God knew what he was doing when he brought you here. This was not a coincidence," he said.

Destiny reluctantly started to believe him. The door of the small room opened. Epic entered with a smile on his face. Spirit followed behind him, latched on to his hand.

"You did it," he said smiling even wider. "She's all good now, and it's because of you."

Destiny was speechless as she stared at Spirit, who did not look Destiny in the eyes. Spirit released Epic's hand and rushed over to Destiny with her head down. She flung her hands around Destiny's neck and held her close.

"Thank you for saving me! I'm so sorry!" Spirit said.

It was the coldest, most haunting hug that Destiny had ever felt. "Jesus," Destiny said in her head. Spirit immediately let go of Destiny's neck and threw her hands up in the air with her eyes closed.

"THANK YA J-SUS!" Spirit yelled.

The Pastor and the ladies in the room began to clap and rejoice. Happiness filled Epic's face. The usher by the door of the small room yelled "Amen" as he, too, clapped his hands. Everyone was convinced that Spirit was healed and delivered; but not Destiny. She was aware of Spirit's performance and refused to entertain it.

The feeling of loneliness came over Destiny all over again as she realized that this was a battle she would have to fight alone. Little did she know that there was an army behind her; we were close behind her.

"Well, you guys come in for what's left of the service. We were just about to do an altar call when y'all joined us," the Pastor said as he guided everyone to the sanctuary.

Destiny unenthusiastically followed the group into the sanctuary. She had a bad feeling in her gut.

"Come on baby, y'all can sit by me," one of the ladies said smiling.

The lady escorted Destiny to an open seat on a center row of the fuchsia-colored pews. The lady cushioned comfortably beside Destiny, picked up an old tambourine, and started banging to the beat of the choir. The lady was on the left side of Destiny; to her right, was Spirit.

Destiny felt like she was watching a play as the choir sang, and people clapped their hands to the beat of the drums. It was all so surreal to her how everyone in the entire congregation was fooled by Spirit's lame act. All she could think about was how, and if, she would ever make it home.

The Pastor got up to address the audience. "Once again," he said into the microphone, "God has shown up and shown out!"

He proceeded to tell the members of the church a brief summary of what happened and how blessed he was to not only have the opportunity to help Spirit, but to also meet his estranged nephew. Destiny listened without reaction. Her mind was not on the Pastor's greeting as she prayed silently in her head.

Out of nowhere, she felt a heavy presence of darkness. She felt a sudden pressure pushing into her chest like something was trying to crush her. Then, there was a blaring roar of laughter in her right ear. Destiny jumped, grabbing her ears in terror. She looked around and everyone was still engaged in what the Pastor was saying. No one had heard what she had heard. Destiny looked over at Spirit only to see the cold black eyes that she had seen before. An evil glare pierced through the tangled black hair hanging in Spirit's face. Destiny jumped out of her seat.

"What's wrong?" the lady to left asked.

"She's not better," Destiny whispered as she tried to leave the pew.

The lady lightly pulled Destiny back down to the bench. This time, she was seated on the opposite side of the lady, away from Spirit, but the presence remained beside her and it was heavier than it was before they had arrived at the church. It did not submit to the church walls – not this church. Instead, it appeared to make it stronger. Destiny was shaken, but not fearful. She refused to submit to the spirit of fear. She made it too far to let it win now.

"You're just traumatized darling," the lady whispered, patting Destiny's leg.

But Destiny knew better. She was far from traumatized.

The Pastor called for those in need of prayer to join him at the altar. Spirit was the first to make her way down. She, who had mastered her role, stood at the altar with her hands uplifted. Destiny watched and listened cautiously. She could still vividly hear the roars of laughter that exited Spirit's soul and clearly entered her ears. Destiny was not at all fooled.

After the service the Pastor pulled Destiny and Epic to the side.

"So what are your plans?" he asked with concern.

"We're going to head back to Houston," Epic answered.

"Well it's too late to drive such a distance as tired as you all are. There is hotel down the road, let me get you three a room so you can lay your head until the morning."

"I don't think that's a good idea," Destiny replied.

Both Pastor Thompson and Epic looked at her with a question mark on their faces. "Why not?" they both asked at the same time.

Destiny looked on the other side of the foyer at Spirit who was still entertaining a small crowd of people.

"Because she's not better," Destiny said with her eyes fixated on Spirit.

"You're just shaken up because of what we've been through, and that's understandable. But she really is doing better," Epic said convincingly.

"You guys really do need rest before getting on that road," the pastor added.

Destiny shook her head and shrugged her shoulders. It was pointless to try and change their minds. It was obvious that they had been fooled by Spirits' trickery. She would have to fight alone.

"Come on. Just follow me," the Pastor said

As the three walked to the car, Spirit stayed as far away from Destiny as she could. She knew that Destiny had identified the truth and felt threatened around her. The car followed the Pastor to the old building down the road from the church. The bright baby light on the top of the building read "Motel," not "Hotel."

"Great," Destiny mumbled as they pulled up in front of the pay office.

The Pastor got out of his red sports car and went into the office. After a few minutes, he looked through the glass door and motioned for Epic to join him.

"I'll be right back, they probably need my I.D." Epic said, opening the car door to get out.

Destiny looked at the back seat where Spirit was sound asleep.

"I'm coming too," she said hopping out of the front seat.

Destiny, Epic, and Pastor Thompson waited for the man behind the counter to type their information into the small gray computer propped on the desk. The pastor fanned his face as the man behind the counter dedicated his every breath to the brown pipe that hung loosely from his mouth.

"I know it's not the best, but this is just so you all can get some rest," the Pastor stated.

Epic looked down at the gold watch on his wrist. "That's only a couple of hours anyway."

Just then, a loud banging noise came from outside. The Pastor and Epic ran to the glass door to see what it was. Destiny followed behind them.

"Oh my goodness," Pastor Thompson said.

"My car!" Epic yelled.

Both men dashed out to the car. The windshield was cracked into a thousand pieces, on the verge of shattering completely. Spirit was in the front seat with her knees arched as her feet violently thumped the glass.

"Let me out of here!" she screamed.

Epic swung the car door open, "What is wrong with you?"

The Pastor was speechless for about thirty seconds before he ran to assist Epic with the now viscous Spirit. Destiny watched with her arms folded as she glared out the glass door from inside the motel office. She was not surprised at what was happening. She knew Spirit was not better. She knew that she had faked her miraculous healing back at Mount Zion. She now knew exactly what was going on.

A half an hour had passed before Epic and the pastor managed to calm Spirit down. Destiny watched closely. The pastor sighed right before opening the glass door of the motel office where Destiny stood motionless.

"You guys definitely need to get her to Houston. She's going to need long term help for her emotional distress. I call it a nervous breakdown."

Destiny listened quietly as the pastor continued. "I prayed with her again, so she should be okay now and I think she will be fine in the morning, too. Just stay prayerful."

"Hold on," Destiny interrupted, "you're going to leave us here? I told you she wasn't better, she just proved it."

"I do agree that she needs help, but there is just no way physically possible that you guys will make it to Houston as tired as you all are."

"I'm not tired," Destiny quickly responded.

Pastor Thompson paused and looked into her bloodshot eyes with disbelief. "You need the rest. You all need the rest," he said calmly.

"Well do we have to stay here? Can't we go to your house?"

"You will be fine," the pastor said, gently placing his hand on Destiny's shoulder.

He grabbed the plastic room key that the clerk had thrown on the counter and walked Destiny out to the car. Destiny saddened as she watched the red sports car drive away from the old motel. The pastor's presence was a warm taste of comfort while it lasted, but now Destiny had to return to her dark world all alone.

Epic flopped on one of the dingy mattresses facedown with his arms extended like an eagle. "I'm so tired," he uttered.

Spirit went into the tiny bathroom to take a shower. Destiny waited until she heard the water running and then went over to the bed where Epic was and slapped the back of his leg.

"What?" he jumped.

"We can't just go to sleep like everything's normal. Can you honestly trust that?" she whispered.

"I don't. But I'm just so tired I can't even think," Epic mumbled as he began to fall asleep.

Destiny slapped him again. "We can't!" she whispered a little louder.

Epic sat up in the bed and rubbed his eyes. "Baby girl," he said softly, "there is no way in hell I can drive like this. There is just no way."

"Well then I'll drive," Destiny said

"Your eyes are as red as mine. It's not safe. We just can't."

Destiny sat on the bed and deeply exhaled.

"Look," he continued, "why don't we take turns sleeping. One of us can sleep while the other keeps an eye on her. All I need is thirty minutes and I'll be good."

Destiny could see his eyes trying to close. "Fine, take a nap but then we leave. I am not sleeping in here with her."

Destiny heard the water in the bathroom stop. The door opened slowly and Spirit came out with the same clothes that she had on before.

"You okay?" Epic asked Spirit

"I'm fine," she answered dryly.

She picked up a brush from the counter beside the bathroom and turned to face the mirror directly above the counter and began brushing her hair with her back turned to Destiny and Epic, who were now looking at each other.

"Just thirty minutes," Epic whispered to Destiny.

Destiny nodded her head and then looked back at the mirror where Spirit stood brushing her tangled black hair. In the reflection of the mirror Destiny's eyes met with the cold black eyes of Spirit. Destiny immediately broke eye contact and nudged Epic's side.

"Why don't you come lay down? You need rest," Epic asked Spirit.

"I know. I'm better now," Spirit responded.

She walked over to the other dingy mattress and nuzzled under the thin plaid blanket. Within seconds she was asleep.

Destiny whispered to Epic, "Thirty minutes," as she stood up and took her position with her back leaned up against the wall next to the door.

Epic was out cold. It felt like minutes before Destiny saw the blanket from the other bed start to move. Spirit abruptly erected from under the blanket and unveiled the cover from her face. Once again, the dark cold eyes maliciously glared at Destiny. Only this time, they were moving towards her.

"Get up!" Destiny yelled tapping Epic on the foot.

He did not hear her. Sprit moved closer.

"Get up!" Destiny yelled again. This time, she hit him on his back.

Epic popped up discombobulated. "What's wrong?" he asked.

Sprit stopped and smiled, still staring at Destiny. "I have to use the restroom." She said cheerfully. She went into the bathroom and closed the door behind her.

"I am not staying here!" Destiny said to Epic

Epic looked at his watch. What seemed like only minutes to Destiny had in reality been two hours.

"It's five o'clock," Epic yawned. "It's time to leave anyway."

He studied the shaken Destiny who stared anxiously at the bathroom door.

"Are you alright?" he asked.

"I'm fine," Destiny responded still staring at the door, "I'll just wait for you guys in the car."

Destiny grabbed the car keys off of the nightstand and went out into the dark to the little silver car. She took her seat on the passenger side and locked the doors. She immediately broke down in tears. "God, I need you!" she cried, "I can't do this without you, oh God!"

In the midst of her tears, Destiny felt the presence of God suddenly rush into the car. It was like a hurricane of wind gushing through her spirit, and along with it came peace. We took our positions and surrounded the little silver car like an army of soldiers. Indeed we were. I reached over and whispered in her ear, "I plead the blood of Jesus," she repeated.

More help came.

By the time Epic and Spirit got to the car, Destiny was at peace. She even managed to take a five-minute catnap. Restoration was in progress. Epic opened the door for Spirit, who slid in the back seat of the car. She initiated another evil stare with Destiny. Her eyes were still cold and black, but they appeared as little harmless marbles to Destiny, who boldly stared back at her. Spirit turned away and cowered into a corner of the back seat. I smiled. They continued their journey to Houston once again. This time, there was no turning back.

14
THE SHIFT

Finally, the little silver car raced down Interstate 45 heading back to Houston. Destiny was relieved to see familiar ground. It was a long and annoying ride as Destiny and Epic suffered through Spirits many personality changes. Spirit made every attempt to have Epic turn the car around. She even stooped to saying that she forgot her favorite brush and that it was imperative that they go back and get it. Spirit tried everything, but Destiny and Epic did not fall for any of her stories.

"So where are we going?" Destiny asked Epic.

"To my Aunt Bev's house. I called her while we were at that church. They're expecting us."

"Does she know…Everything?" Destiny asked.

"Baby girl, I come from a long line of prayer warriors. I never thought I'd be sharing this with you, but I do. If there's anybody prepared for this kind of stuff, it's my auntie."

"Good," Destiny replied.

The closer and closer the car got to Auntie's house, the more uncomfortable Spirit became. Her actions were no longer intimidating – it was obvious that the powers within her had weakened. She was more nervous than anything. Epic pulled up to the long driveway of his aunt's house; his aunt and her husband were standing on the porch waiting.

Destiny couldn't wait to get out of the car. She did not know Epic's aunt, but she was overly relieved to see her. The aunt welcomed her with a warm hug. It was as though Destiny had met with civilization for the very first time. She led Destiny into the house and up a set of stairs to a secluded den area. It was the most peaceful room Destiny had ever been in. Epic and the husband got Spirit out of the car and took her to a separate room.

"I heard it's been a long week," Aunt Bev said to Destiny, handing her a glass of ice tea.

"Yes ma'am," Destiny responded, taking a sip of the glass.

Aunt Bev smiled at Destiny without words. She did not ask any questions, she just remained quiet as Destiny sipped her tea. Epic entered the room.

"Wow!" he said with a sigh of relief.

"How is she?" Aunt Bev asked.

"It's like she slipped into a coma after your husband put that oil on her. She's fast asleep."

"They can't stay awake here, they know better than that," Aunt Bev said as she looked over at Destiny, staring directly into her eyes.

Destiny felt a quiver run down her spine as she took another sip of her tea. She found it strange that Epic's aunt wasn't asking a million questions about their ordeal as she had expected. Aunt Bev didn't ask what the three were doing in Dallas in the first place, she didn't ask for any details – she didn't ask anything! Instead, she just sat there staring at Destiny with a pleasant smile on her face.

"Come here son," Aunt Bev said to Epic, finally breaking her silence.

The two went into the hallway. Destiny could hear them go down the stairs and out the front door. Destiny put the remainder of her ice tea on a small round table next to her. She put both hands on her face and let out a long sigh. Her mind scattered, trying to grasp a hold of reality. She could not believe what she had just been through, and more importantly, she could not believe that she made it out alive.

Epic and his aunt returned to the secluded den area where Destiny sat indulging the peaceful atmosphere.

"You ready to go baby girl?" Epic asked

"Yes, I need to get to my kids."

"Sweetheart, you need to take some time to regroup before you get those babies – at least a day or two," Aunt Bev said gently.

"But I haven't seen them in two weeks, I have to!" Destiny argued.

Aunt Bev took a few steps towards Destiny and reached for her hands. With her big hazel-colored eyes, she looked deep into the eyes of Destiny. "Baby, trust me. Not now," she said gently.

"I suppose you're right," Destiny replied.

Destiny had not even noticed that she had jerked her hands away from the petite, light-skinned woman. I extended my hands towards Destiny also. I agreed that it was a bad idea for her to be around her children in the condition that she was in.

Aunt Bev led Destiny and Epic back downstairs and outside to the porch. Epic handed Destiny the car keys and asked her to wait in the car while he said goodbye to his Auntie. Aunt Bev gave Destiny a long warm hug that made Destiny's heart rate awkwardly increase. Again, without realizing Destiny quickly broke loose from the hug and went to the car.

Destiny could tell that Epic and his aunt were hiding something from Destiny, but she did not spend much time thinking about all of the possibilities. They were probably talking about Spirit anyway. Although Destiny felt terrible for Spirit, she did not mind if she never laid eyes on her again.

Destiny waited patiently in the car for Epic to finish his conversation with his aunt. She watched as their lips moved rapidly; occasionally they would glance in the direction of the little silver car. It was eleven o'clock on a Saturday morning and the neighborhood kids started coming outside to play. Destiny looked out of the window and watched a freckle-faced little boy chase a little girl with curly pig tails around in circles. It looked like he had some sort of gooey substance in his hand. Destiny smiled. The more signs of normal civilization she saw, the better she felt. She took a deep sigh of relief and looked back to the porch.

All of a sudden, she saw a dark silhouette appear behind Epic and his aunt. It was Spirit; behind her was the aunt's husband trying to pull her back into the house. Epic and his aunt assisted in getting the zombie-like being back inside the house. Destiny gulped and her skin started to crawl. Epic, his aunt, and his uncle managed to detain Spirit, but not before she administered a deadly ogle with Destiny. Their eyes interlocked as she bore deep into Destiny's soul. Destiny tried hard to break eye contact, but she could not move. She felt frozen. Spirit smiled and then surrendered and went into the house voluntarily. Something happened.

Destiny felt fear suffocating her all over again. She snatched her cellphone from off her lap and dialed a number. This time she made sure it was her own mother. Like a baby, the only thing Destiny wanted at that very moment was to be consoled by her mom.

"Hello," her mother answered.

"Mom, it's me," Destiny said hesitantly

"I know. Where have you been?"

"In Dallas and the most awful thing happened. I'll tell you about it later, but right now I need you to tell me what to do," Destiny said almost in tears.

"About what?" her mom asked.

"Well, you know how grandma always used to tell us stories about how she had to fight off demons and spirits? How she could see them in people?"

"Yes."

"Well I think I'm going through that right now, and I don't know what to do." Destiny began to hyperventilate.

"Well how did you get yourself in that situation anyway? And what were you doing in Dallas? It's the crowd of people you choose to hang around, of course, they're all full of demons. You should learn how to choose your friends more wisely…"

Destiny silently listened to her mothers' lecture as she went on to tell Destiny how disappointed she was. All that Destiny wanted was someone to pray with her without judgment. Out of all the people Destiny knew, she was sure her mother would support her no matter what, but she was wrong. Instead, her mother turned out to be her worst critic.

Destiny realized that it was fate that she accidently dialed Vision's mother during her breakdown in Dallas. If her own mother had answered, she may not have made it back to Houston. Her mother was still on the phone venting and Destiny could feel herself get weaker and weaker as the stones drilled through the phone.

"I'll call you back," Destiny said politely.

"Where are you going now? Where are the kids?" her mother asked with an attitude.

"I'll call you back," Destiny repeated.

Epic finally came outside of the house and jogged to the car.

"I'm sorry about that," he said getting into the car. He buckled his seatbelt and started the engine. "Okay, so where to? You should probably…" He paused as he looked over at Destiny who had been crying. "What's the matter?" he asked.

"I'm fine," Destiny said, wiping her face.

"Are you sure? What happened?" he asked unconvinced.

"Nothing, I'm fine. I guess I'm still shaken up, that's all."

"Of course," he said compassionately. "That's why I was thinking that I should take you to your mom's house. That's probably the best place for you right now before you go home to your kids."

"I can't go there," Destiny said firmly.

"Why? I think you need to be with your family…"

"I can't!" Destiny yelled.

"Okay. Well you can stay with me," he said softly.

Destiny nodded.

"I have to go the hospital and fill out some paper work, but first we need to get some clothes, and then some sleep."

"You mean the crazy house?" Destiny asked.

Epic giggled, "Yeah, I guess you can call it that. I need to give them some information to get her processed. Until then, she's going to stay with my aunt."

Destiny was silent. Out of everything that she had gone through with Spirit, the most vivid memory was the chilling stare that she had encountered just moments ago. It was unlike the others. It was not just a dark and cold stare, it was intense and had meaning behind it. Destiny could not figure out what it meant, but she knew it was not good. She began to feel strange and discombobulated. She felt like she was losing control of her mind and her emotions. She felt timid and lost. She felt death. Destiny did not mention to Epic what she was feeling – she didn't have to. He, too, saw something different about her.

Since Destiny and Epic had left all of their luggage back in Dallas, they stopped and got a couple of outfits from a local department store before heading to the hospital. The only things that Destiny was able to grab were her purse and some white rubber flip flops. She had on a white t-shirt and some blue jean shorts, and her hair was a mess. Destiny hadn't noticed until now how terrible she looked. Epic drove to the neighborhood where his studio was.

"We can change over here," he said pulling in front of the pale yellow house.

The pair was greeted by Epic's entourage, who stood outside puffing on their cigarettes as usual. Zee, the driver, was amongst them.

"What's up?" one of them shouted.

"Welcome to Houston," another hollered.

"Here, you can go in the studio and change. I'll go after you," Epic said handing Destiny a small bag of clothes as they walked past the small crowd.

"Oh and let me get the toothbrushes," he said turning back towards the car.

"I am not brushing my teeth here," Destiny whispered in disgust.

Epic laughed. "Okay, well go change. I'll be in there in a second."

Destiny paused. There was a pulling inside of her that did not want to leave Epic's side. She felt excessively drawn to him for some reason, and the very thought of separation even for a moment frightened her.

He noticed her stalling and repeated, "I'll be in there in a second."

Destiny opened the side door that was hanging off of its hinges, walked through the pest-infested kitchen, and down the dark moldy hallway. She locked the studio door behind her and changed her clothes as fast as she could. She swung open the studio door and there stood the old lady of the house, Miss Terry. Destiny was startled.

"You okay, Slim?"

"Yes ma'am," Destiny answered timidly – everything seemed to startle her now. "How are you?"

"Oh I'm fine. You sure you alright?" Miss Terry asked again.

"I'm sure," Destiny responded. Miss Terry was the last person Destiny would share her terrifying story with.

"I overheard them boys talking outside. Something about somebody gone crazy. Are you gone crazy, Slim?"

Destiny shook her head, speechless.

"Well I hope not," Miss Terry said, "I wouldn't want to see you crazy. You already tied to evil."

"What do you mean, Miss Terry?" Destiny asked.

"Your soul, it's tied up to that there boy. He got you."

"I really have to go Miss Terry," Destiny said walking passed the old lady.

"You have to break that soul-tie before it brings you down – straight to hell is where it'll have you. I know. They almost got me too."

Destiny increased her pace. She was anxious to get away from the delusional old lady. She heard enough psychotic talk for the week and didn't want to entertain anymore of it. The lazy old dog lying on the floor popped his head up as Destiny approached the kitchen. Even he looked strange to Destiny. Destiny felt herself get jumpy and everything in sight began to frighten her. She bolted through the side door and ran down the dirt-filled driveway. Epic was alarmed to see the horror on her face.

"What's happened," he asked dropping his cigarette to the ground.

"Can we leave?" Destiny asked as her voice cracked.

"Sure. Come on, I'll change clothes later." He shook hands with his entourage and followed Destiny to the car.

Epic waited a good ten minutes before questioning Destiny. It was evident that something had her shaken up.

"Did Miss Terry say something to upset you?" he finally asked.

Destiny shook her head no.

"Okay, I'm just checking."

Epic was quiet as he calculated his thoughts. Destiny didn't utter a word either. Before getting to the hospital, Epic pulled into an empty parking lot of a big white church, not far from his studio inside the raggedy yellow house.

"This is my Auntie's church," he said smiling. "This is where every generation of prayer warriors in my family went. This is where I grew up. Can you believe it?"

Destiny was unaware that she was leaned over to the drivers' seat holding on to Epic's arm for dear life. She squeezed tightly as he drove closer to the actual building. She was shaking and her head felt like it was spinning in circles. Epic looked over at her and observed her reactions. He had driven to the church grounds on purpose, and for that very reason. "Aunt Bev was right," he whispered to himself as Destiny clung to his arm with her eyes closed.

He drove away from the church and out of the parking lot. Destiny instantly regained her composure. She was uncertain of what had just taken place, but she knew that she wasn't herself. Something was wrong. She looked at Epic, "Please don't let it get me too. Please. You can't leave me."

"I won't," he said, "I'm here."

15

THE WIN

Destiny and Epic arrived at the hospital for the mentally ill. Upon entering the building, Destiny began to hear unknown voices inside of her head. Low risk patients wandered around outside and in the lobby, some having intellectual conversations with themselves, while others were playing card games. They were no threat to society, but Destiny could see past their good behavior. She could see the spirits that flocked around their heads, tormenting them with confusion. She heard the voices cream profanities, begging the spirits to leave them alone. It was as though Destiny had something in common with these people as she identified their demons.

"Did you hear me?" Epic asked, trying to get Destiny's attention.

"Huh?" Destiny responded. She hadn't noticed that Epic was speaking to her. She could not hear beyond the voices in her head.

"I said that is it for now. All I had to do was fill out the paper work and they'll go get her tomorrow."

"Oh ok," Destiny responded.

Epic recognized the blank look on Destiny's face – he had seen it before. "Come on. Let's go get some rest," he said, putting his arm around her shoulder.

After driving through a fast food restaurant, Epic drove to a fancy motel.

"I don't think I can stay in another hotel, or motel!" Destiny said in a panic as the little silver car pulled up in front of the motel.

"I live with my mother, you don't want to go to your mother's, you can't go home to your kids right now, the studio is a trash can – this is our only option, baby girl."

Destiny looked up at the four-story building and sighed grudgingly.

"We'll be fine, baby girl. You literally haven't slept in two days, you need the rest."

"I guess," Destiny shrugged.

Epic paid for the room and the two headed up a flight of stairs to the fifth floor where their room was. They ate the burgers they had gotten from the fast food joint and then showered. The room was facing the street and Destiny could hear cars zooming past. It was cold and the old air conditioning unit roared loudly.

The multi-colored carpet had water stains around its perimeter, the popcorn textured walls were a neutral color, similar to an off-white or beige, and there was only one bed with a small nightstand next to it which held a little dim lamp that flickered periodically. Beside the lamp was a black Bible, which looked like it hadn't been touched in ages. The blankets were a soft mauve color and were exceptionally soft for it to be property of the motel. The bathroom was clean and painted in the purest of whites, and contained a pure white toilet, pure white bathtub, and a pure white sink. Even the countertop in the small bathroom was pure white.

"Come on, let's get some sleep. I don't ever remember being this tired!" Epic said getting into the bed.

Destiny threw the fast food bags in the trash and nestled beside him.

"I've never been to bed this early either," he said as he placed his cellphone on the small nightstand.

"I'm scared," Destiny whispered.

"I know," Epic replied, "I got you."

The two cuddled and dozed off to sleep.

The temperature in the room had dropped. The thermostat read forty-nine degrees Fahrenheit. A slender ray of sunlight beamed from behind the blinds covering the windows. The sounds of cars racing down the street could vaguely be heard over the roar of the blasting AC unit and birds chirped harmoniously by the window.

The little lamp on the nightstand flickered, but this time the light did not return. I waited patiently as I brushed my wings over the black dusty Bible sitting on the nightstand. I traced my fingers over several scriptures, but left it open to one in particular. I smiled as I read over it. Psalms 91 verse 11 had been manifested, *"For He will order His angels to protect you wherever you go."* It was time to go to war. I took my position.

"NOOOOO!" Destiny screeched, jolting from a deep slumber.

Her eyes were deliriously bulged out of her head, her back was arched backwards, and her hands were ejected as her fingers clawed at Epic's face. Through Destiny's eyes was the image of Epic's tongue in the form of a serpent flying out of his mouth towards her. To her, his eyes were the same eyes she had seen in Spirit, but ten times more evil. His body appeared to be in a gyrating motion, confusing Destiny of his exact whereabouts.

"NOOOOO!" she screamed again, brutally intensifying her attack of self-defense.

Epic desperately tried to gain control of her hands. "Destiny!" he yelled.

This seemed to terrify her even more as she was now using her feet to aid in her aggressive attack.

He yelled out for her attention, but this time by her birth name. Immediately, her screaming stopped and she was no longer kicking and scratching. She looked into the face of Epic and realized who he really was. The serpent tongue was no longer there and his face was now recognizable.

"What's happening?" she asked frantically. "What's happening?"

"You're going to be okay," Epic said reaching for his phone.

"No I'm not!" Destiny yelled. "It's happening to me, too! I have to stop it!"

Destiny bolted towards the door of the five story building and headed straight for the balcony. "I have to stop it!" she screamed again. She perched the upper portion of her body against the rail of the balcony and attempted to swing herself over. "I have to stop it!" she said one last time.

Epic grabbed the back of her shirt just in time and pulled her back into the room. Destiny was somewhat aware of what was going on – it was like she would leave her body and then jump right back in. One minute Epic looked normal and the next minute he looked like a disfigured beast trying to devour her. Her flesh was weak. It was like she was in a boxing match with herself, like her spirit was fighting against her soul. Indeed, there was a fight.

"Call…" Destiny began to say, struggling to get the words out of her mouth. She could feel her tongue rolling to the back of her throat. "Call help," she managed to let out. "My phone," she said falling to the floor.

Epic ran to the nightstand and snatched her phone. He glanced down at the black dusty Bible that was now open. He knew for a fact that the Bible was closed before they went to bed. He scanned over the verse that I had subliminally highlighted.

"I got your phone. Who should I call?"

"Cousin," Destiny uttered before going to another state of illusion.

Epic scrolled through her list of contacts and found the first name that had the word "cousin" in parenthesis. A woman answered. He had no time to get her name as he immediately gave her a rapid introduction and proceeded to tell her what was going on. Meanwhile, Destiny was flopping around on the floor screaming obscenities like, "I hate myself" and "I need to die." She scratched her arms until she drew blood, yelling, "I'm filthy. I'm garbage."

Epic went over to Destiny who was lying helplessly on the floor and put the cell phone to her ear.

"Can you hear me?" her cousin asked, calling Destiny by her birth name.

Destiny snapped out of a near catatonic state and listened to her cousin.

"Listen honey, I need you to sing! Do hear you me! You worship as loud as you can and don't stop!"

Destiny's tongue unfolded as she bolted out songs of worship. Still in the midst, something would overtake her and her tongue locked up, folding to the back of her throat. "I hate myself!" Destiny hollered as her body slammed against the wall.

Epic put the phone back to his ear.

"Okay I will keep you posted," Epic said to the cousin, and then hung up the phone.

He waited until Destiny snapped back to her normal self and then escorted her into the all-white bathroom.

"Your cousin said it's best to be by white," he said, closing the bathroom door. "Who else should I call?"

"Grandma," Destiny mumbled from behind the door.

Epic got Destiny's grandmother on the phone and told the story once again. The grandmother could hear Destiny's horrifying screams and loud banging noises in the background as Destiny's body flew into the walls and against the bathtub. It sounded like there were ten people in the small restroom, all engaged in a vicious rumble.

Immediately, the grandmother broke into a powerful prayer. She prayed and prayed and prayed. She prayed healing, she prayed deliverance, and she prayed restoration, all while speaking in a different tongue; powerful, mighty tongue. Though she lived a long distance from Houston, her prayers were up-close and personal. Epic put the phone on speaker and held it up to the bathroom door. The banging noises ceased. This time, help came from every region. I took my stance as I greeted them – the war was almost over.

After her prayers, the grandmother instructed Epic to contact Destiny's oldest brother, Roger, who also resided in Houston. He had never met him before, but he did not waste any time calling him.

Destiny sat behind the bathroom door balled up in a corner between the door and the bathtub. She ripped at her ears trying to silence the death threats in her head. Her tongue was still stuck in a folded position at the back of her throat, and she felt herself slowly losing air.

There was a knock on the bathroom door, and then it opened. Destiny's eyes saw a bright blinding light surrounding an image of her older brother. She squinted her eyes tightly, trying to block the blazing light that had entered the bathroom.

"Jesus," the deep voice said.

Destiny jumped as Roger's hand came towards her.

"Come on sis," he said.

In her heart, Destiny wanted so desperately to reach out and grab her brother's hand, but something in her mind would not allow her to accept his warm invitation. Roger moved closer to Destiny and grabbed her hand. Destiny's body flew into a supernatural tantrum as it revolted backwards off of the floor, like she was a gymnast moving about in thin air. Voices, different voices, squealed from out of her mouth warning her brother to let her go. He was far from shaken. He pulled Destiny to her feet and carried her out of the bathroom and into the room.

"No weapon formed against me shall prosper," he said firmly looking Destiny directly in her eyes.

She quivered and pulled her hand away from him. The front door was wide open and she cowardly ran to the corner beside the bed to try and shield the glaring sunlight that pierced through the room. She peaked at the images surrounding her. There stood Roger and his wife, Cheryl. They appeared to be wearing halos on their heads, and a peaceful light beamed from their eyes. Behind them stood Epic in deep observation.

Roger picked up the black dusty Bible from off of the nightstand and smiled as he noticed the scripture that I had highlighted. He began reading verses from the same scripture and then flipped to Psalms 91. His voice was firm and clear as he read aloud, with his eyes set on Destiny. His wife went over to Destiny and touched her on her back. Destiny jumped.

"You don't know what I've done," Destiny fought to utter the words. "I deserve this, I'm filthy."

"I rebuke that in the name of Jesus," Cheryl responded. "You are fearfully and wonderfully made! You are a child of the Most High God! You are made in His image and His likeness!"

"No!" a voice screamed from Destiny's mouth, "My name is Destiny and I am worthless!"

Cheryl continued to profess, "You're name is NOT Destiny! That is a street name from your past. You are God's child DESTINED for greatness!"

Cheryl repeatedly called her sister-in-law by her true name, her birth name. The Destined could taste blood in her mouth as her teeth bore into her tongue. Her lips snapped together, trapping her words. She tried to fight it, but had no control over it. Roger put the Bible down and walked over to his vulnerable sister huddled in the corner.

"Call his name sis, call on Jesus!" he said softly.

The Destined tried, but her mouth would not move. She felt her tongue burrow deeper into her throat.

"Call Him for your children, call on the name of JESUS!" he said again.

A picture of her kids flashed through the mind of the Destined. She fought against the forces trying to bind her tongue and managed to utter the word, "Jesus."

"Again," Roger said.

"Jesus!" she repeated a little louder.

Her tongue slowly unfolded. The precious name came out of her lips without struggle.

"Jesus! Jesus! Jesus!" she said repeatedly. She was no longer just repeating after her brother. The Destined was now rejoicing. The battle was over.

There was a sudden peace that filled the atmosphere. Though the room felt physically hot and clammy, the windows fogged and the ground was cold. The roaring whisper of the cheap air conditioning unit was at last the only sound that roared. The little lamp on the nightstand flickered dimly, and the sun tried to peek through the foggy windows, but it was dark. The eyes of the audience glanced around the room in an overwhelming state of shock, but amongst them was peace – a sudden calmness.

It was there that The Destined laid balled into a fetal position, her knees pressed firmly against her chin, her nails digging into the dorsal part of both hands as they anxiously clenched together. Tears streamed from her eyes, following the dried patterns of a previous outpour. Her face was so sticky that it itched. Her tongue was swollen, and her voice was hoarse, as though she had been screaming for days, for months, for years! The band of voices had fled from the innermost parts of her brain; there was only one now. Her ears unclogged, her vision returned. She lifted her head and blankly studied the crowd of three that had gathered in amazement. Her blurry pupils traced the ray of sunlight that pierced through the foggy window. She exhaled. The uninvited, once bold and intimidating, realized that they had no place and left. The door abruptly closed behind them. She was herself again.

"Thank you!" the Destined whimpered with a smile on her face. Her flesh was weak, but she felt an amazing rush of strength within her spirit.

"Don't thank me. Thank Jehovah" Roger said laughing.

Destiny smiled and looked towards the sky and said, "Thank you, Jesus."

"We'll take her with us," Cheryl told Epic.

Epic agreed without argument. He, too, was relieved.

The Destined, previously known as Destiny, paused in her tracks and glanced back at Epic.

"Goodbye … Eric," she said weakly.

"Goodbye… Kate," he smiled.

"So who are you?" Roger asked his sister as they headed down the stairs to his car.

"I am fearfully and wonderfully made. I am a child of God, DESTINED for greatness!" she said boldly. Her knees wobbled from weakness, but she felt renewed.

"And what's your name?" Cheryl asked.

"My name is Kate," she answered with a huge smile.

"…and who is Destiny?" Roger asked.

Kate stopped to think about her response. She sighed, and then smiled.

"That person doesn't exist anymore" she said courageously.

Kate's brother put his arm around his sister's shoulders and embraced her in a hug.

"Thank you Jesus," he whispered.

Eric stood on the steps leading to the room as he watched Kate leave with her family. It was uncertain what his future would hold, but he knew that it would not include her. The naive, vulnerable girl that he named Destiny no longer existed. Her true Destiny was beyond his imagination. He knew that their bond had been broken, and their souls were no longer tied. He was regretful for what he had put her through, but he was happy – happy that she had the chance to become something greater. She was destined for greatness.

I and those that had come to this battle rejoiced in victory. I was one happy angel as I watched my assignment drive away with her loved ones. I looked to the sky and praised His holy name. What a rewarding assignment this was indeed! He never ceases to amaze me. My God; again, He prevails. Again, His power is revealed.

Though the war was far from over, The Destined was back where she belonged – in the loving arms of her Heavenly Father.

16

THE REVELATION

Spirits, angels, demons, strange voices controlling the logic of the sound mind, unexplained forces, unseen to the natural eye. Could there be a scientific theory for such an emotionally driven imagination? Could such a fictional string of events ever prove to be reality to earthly beings? Maybe not. But then again, maybe so.

Destiny was an ordinary girl. She was not a super hero and did not have any supernatural powers – she was a girl whose brokenness led her to choices unimaginable to her own comprehension of life. The desire to be loved burrowed deep into her soul and created an emptiness she did not recognize. Blinded by her own insecurities, Destiny searched desperately to feel needed, loved, and complete. Overshadowed by shame and regret, she desired simply to exist – to be acknowledged as acceptable, no matter where that validation came from.

Though you may not be a "Destiny," you do have a story and each day represents a page of your life. Some may have the perfect cover, but some of their pages are torn – the story continues anyway. Some of the pages in this book were unimaginable and probably hard to digest, but Destiny's story continued anyway. No matter what life brings to you (or you bring to it), it's never too late as long as your story is still being written.

My name is Katherine, otherwise known as Destiny. I am a mother, author, writer, and mentor. Whether this book speaks to you from a realistic point of view or not, my prayer is that somewhere within this story, you will find a piece of yourself. Perhaps you, too, have lived with an emptiness hidden behind things that provide temporary comfort. Or maybe you've never addressed certain things in your life that cause you to 'act out of character' – or you've accepted the unacceptable because it's been a part of you for so long. Could it be that your smile is the glue that keeps you from falling apart at times?

I grew up in a single-parent household. I knew my father well, but he wasn't there. Though I was unaware at the time, I longed to fill a void that my father took when he left. I longed to be loved – an insecure little girl whose only self-respect came from the validation of others. I had no confidence, no trust, and no identity. I did not know who I was or who I was created to be. Even as a young child, I can remember doing things only to please others. I was lost and did not like who I was. I felt as though I did not belong. These were feelings that I disguised so well. I hid my insecurities in things that were artificial – fake friendships, fake relationships, fake attitudes, etc. Please know, a smile does not always indicate happiness. Those closest to me had no way of knowing what I was feeling or how thirsty I was to be accepted and loved– at least my view of love at the time.

I went through the events written in this book. I am grateful for an experience that brought me to my knees and showed me exactly who I was and who I was made to be. I am grateful for an experience that caused me to nearly lose my mind, and my life. Am I proud of it? Absolutely not. However, if I would have never gone through it, if I would have never fallen so far beneath my character, how then would I know who I was created to be? Everyone has a story, and yes, my story may be looked down upon – a promiscuous, insecure little girl with no self-respect. But I am ecstatic for the opportunity to share it. Sometimes we go through things in life that put us in a position to help others. Everyone who reads this may not share the same struggle as I did, but everyone reading this has a story. *You* have a story. Whether good or bad, your story is being written – it's your tool to help others. For me, my tool is used to show others that no matter what you've been through, your past does not define who you are. I am no longer that insecure little girl. I now know who I am, and I can honestly say that I love myself. God is the true Author of my book, and only *He* can end it. Until then, I will continue to press towards my calling with no regrets, and it's important for you to do the same. It's not how you start the race, it's how you finish.

Underneath the filth, underneath the darkness, God saw a jewel worthy of being saved. He cleaned me up, and here I am today sharing my testimony with you – the forgotten, the unappreciated, the unnoticed, the overachieved in hopes of feeling achieved, the hurt, the broken, the confused, the lost, the embarrassed, and the outcast. If you are reading this, then your story has not ended. Trust the *Author* and *He'll* keep writing.

You never know why someone is in the position they are in, how they got there, or better yet, who they have been called to be. Your tears may look different than the tears of someone else. Love them anyway, no exceptions.

I pray that this message has reached the core of your heart. No more plastic smiles, no more masks – be who you have been created to be.

This is my story. The unspoken has been revealed.

ACKNOWLEDGEMENTS

Mom – You raised me the best way you could. If not for the foundation you laid, I would have been lost. You worked tirelessly to provide for your children and set your own dreams aside so that we could aspire to be what we were created to be. You saw through the pain, hurt, anger, and sadness and loved us anyway. You were overlooked and underappreciated but still, you did not break. If not for you, I would not know how to be as independent as I am today. You prepared us for the real world, all while protecting us from the struggles that came with it. Your love is the epitome of love unconditional. You are truly a wonderful mother, and I thank God for you! I love you more than you will ever know!

Mrs. Terry Simon – If not for you, this story would have a different ending. In the midst of one of the most vulnerable moments of my life, God sent you. That alone speaks volumes of the wisdom, love, and compassion that you have for others. He chose you that day and as we know, only few are chosen. Your obedience will never be forgotten or overlooked. I love you, and I thank you.

Robert and Karen McGibbon – True ANGELS. You were obedient and you were there when I needed you the most. Thank you! Love you.

Larry Green (Dad) – Thank you for stepping in and being just who you are – dad. I cannot express enough how much your constant encouragement and words of affirmation mean to me. You saw something in me that I didn't see in myself. No matter what I did, you pushed me to be better. You spoke highly of me and told me how great I would be – even when you knew I was doing wrong – and you still do! "Kat, I'm so proud of you." You'll never know how much those words mean to me coming from you. I love you.

MeMe Johnson – Your friendship is one of the few things that I value most in this world. When I'm down, you stand for me. When I'm weak, you encourage me. When I'm happy, you smile with me. When others walked away, you were still there. What we have is greater than friendship. What we have is a bond ordained by God that no one can break – not even us! I do not know what I did to deserve such an amazing person to call my best friend, but I thank God for placing you in my life and in my heart. Thank you for always supporting me. I'm so glad we are in this thing called life together. I love you more than you will ever know. HUGS

Mrs. Edna Washington Turner – God positions the right people at the right time. I may fall, but there is no staying down on your watch! Your prayers, your words of encouragement, and your realness remind me of who I am and who I was destined to be. Thank you for your love and acceptance through it all. I love you.

Kayla Tennison – I tell you my dream, you support me. I ask for help, you do not hesitate. I look in my corner, and you are one of the few faces that I see. Your friendship is consistent and I am grateful. Your work is not unnoticed. Love you sis.

Denzel and Jasmine – My "other kids"– read this and know that you can do anything! No matter what life throws your way. Auntie loves you more than I can ever express!

Kierra, Jordan, and Peyton – My world, my everything! You three keep pushing me to be better. What an honor it is to be able to call myself your mother. You are my lifeline and I couldn't imagine life without you. God trusted me enough to bless me with three of his most precious angels, whom I love more than anything in this world. As long as I have you, I will never stop. My babies, I love you more than words, and as our stories multiply, know that they are because of you. Muuaaah!

Blinded by the fear of your past, your soul lays motionless.
In an attempt to revive the spirit that once smiled,
the beats of your heart race against your mind.
The trickery that resides there continue to outshine
who you really are.

You've become a chameleon as your audience chooses which mask
looks best, a stranger to yourself - a victim of identity theft.

Stuck in tracks you've already trailed, stamping grades on tests
you've failed, your soul lays motionless.

But once the play ends and the stage is clear, the costumes are
removed and your soul is bare, maybe then you will see …
who you really are.

Once upon a time does not last forever.

Sincerely,

Kathy